iPads in the Early Years

Digital devices, such as smartphones and tablet computers, are becoming commonplace in young children's lives for play, entertainment, learning and communication. Recently, there has been a great deal of focus on the educational potential of these devices in both formal and informal educational settings. There is now an abundance of educational 'apps' available to children, parents and teachers, which claim to enhance children's early literacy and numeracy development, but to date, there has been very little formal investigation of the educational potential of these devices.

This book discusses the impact on children's learning when iPads were introduced in three very different early years settings in Brisbane, Australia. It outlines how researchers worked with preschool teachers and parents to explore how iPads can assist with letter and word recognition, the development of oral literacy and digital literacies, and talk around play. Chapters consider the possibilities for using iPads for creativity and arts education through photography, storytelling, drawing, music creation and audio recording, and critically examine the literacies enabled by educational software available on iPads, and the relationship between digital play and literacy development.

iPads in the Early Years provides exciting insights into children's digital culture and learning in the age of the iPad. It will be key reading for researchers, research students and teacher educators focusing on the early years, as well as those with an interest in the role of ICTs, and particularly tablet computers, in education.

Michael Dezuanni is Deputy Director of the Children and Youth Research Centre, and a Senior Lecturer in the Creative Industries Faculty and Faculty of Education, Queensland University of Technology, Australia.

Karen Dooley is Associate Professor at Queensland University of Technology, Australia.

Sandra Gattenhof is Associate Professor and Head of Drama in the Creative Industries Faculty, Queensland University of Technology, Australia.

Linda Knight is Senior Lecturer in the Faculty of Education, Queensland University of Technology, Australia.

Routledge Research in Early Childhood Education

This series provides a platform for researchers to present their latest research and discuss key issues in early childhood education.
Books in the series include:

Children as Citizens
Engaging with the child's voice in educational settings
Pauline Harris and Harry Manatakis

Early Years Second Language Education
International perspectives on theory and practice
Edited by Sandie Mourão and Mónica Lourenço

iPads in the Early Years
Developing literacy and creativity
Michael Dezuanni, Karen Dooley, Sandra Gattenhof and Linda Knight

iPads in the Early Years

Developing literacy and creativity

**Michael Dezuanni,
Karen Dooley,
Sandra Gattenhof
and Linda Knight**

Routledge
Taylor & Francis Group
LONDON AND NEW YORK

First published 2015
by Routledge
2 Park Square, Milton Park, Abingdon, Oxfordshire OX14 4RN

and by Routledge
711 Third Avenue, New York, NY 10017

First issued in paperback 2016

Routledge is an imprint of the Taylor & Francis Group, an informa business

British Library Cataloguing in Publication Data
A catalogue record for this book is available from the British Library

Library of Congress Cataloging in Publication Data
iPads in the early years: developing literacy and creativity/Michael Dezuanni, Karen Dooley, Sandra Gattenhof, and Linda Knight.
pages cm
Includes bibliographical references and index.
1. Computers and children. 2. Computer literacy. 3. Education–Data processing. 4. iPad (Computer) I. Dezuanni, Michael.
QA76.9.C659I63 2015
004.083 – dc23
2014030948

ISBN 13: 978-1-138-21973-1 (pbk)
ISBN 13: 978-1-138-77858-0 (hbk)

Typeset in Galliard and Gill Sans
by Florence Production Ltd, Stoodleigh, Devon, UK

Contents

Preface

According to Apple Corporation, sometime in mid-2014 the number of apps available in its App Store exceeded 1.2 million and the number of app downloads was 75 billion. Apple's 'iPad in Education' marketing also tells us there are over 75,000 education apps available. In these numerical terms, at least, the iPad is extremely popular and its apps potentially provide educators with an expansive new resource for use in the classroom. What kind of resource is the iPad, though, and how can it most effectively be used in education? What kinds of apps are best for teaching and learning and how can teachers and students use iPads to develop knowledge and skills? Is the iPad an appropriate learning device for very young children and does it have any place in play-based learning environments? We set out to explore these questions during the course of a year as we investigated children's use of the iPad in early education settings. We were particularly interested in young children's development of literacy and creativity with the iPads. As you will see from the accounts throughout this book we do believe iPads can play a productive role in young children's education. Effective use of the iPads is, though, accompanied by a range of complex pedagogical, technical, social and professional challenges that should not be underestimated. Our aim in this book is to explore these complexities about iPad use in early education and to contribute to the rich dialogue about the educational uses of technology with young children.

Our research would not have been possible without the support of a range of people and organisations. This project originated within Queensland University of Technology's (QUT's) *Children and Youth Research Centre* (www.cyrc.qut.edu.au) under the leadership of the centre's director, Professor Kerry Mallan, who provided generous advice and support throughout the project. We are also highly indebted to Karleen Gwinner who provided research assistance, Jill Nalder who looked after our budget and Geoff Gillan for his project management advice and manuscript preparation support. The project was funded by the Ian Potter Foundation – one of Australia's major philanthropic organisations – and QUT's Equity Division. We also received financial support from the Faculty of Education and Creative Industries Faculty at QUT.

Our key partner in this project was the Gowrie, Queensland. The Gowrie has over 70 years of experience caring for and educating young children in Australia. The Gowrie, Queensland is a community-based, non-profit organisation that currently manages 75 community kindergartens (preschools) and it was with the support of the organisation's Chief Executive Office, Jane Bourne, that we were able to undertake our research in three of the Gowrie's centres. We are highly indebted to our three co-investigators, the Directors of the community kindergartens in which we undertook the research; the support of these three highly professional educators and their colleagues was vital to the success of the project. The children and families in each of the three centres were also very generous with their time and interest in the project and we feel absolutely privileged to have been welcomed into their lives.

Finally, we would like to thank our families and loved ones for their patience and support during the long hours it took to write this book.

Introduction

iPads in the early years: developing literacy and creativity

The iPad is the most successful tablet computer in today's marketplace and it has received a great deal of attention for its potential as a resource for education in both formal settings – like schools and universities – and informal spaces such as the family home. The accessibility of the iPad as an 'easy-to-use' device has led to a great deal of interest from early years educators and young children's parents and caregivers who have watched with a degree of amazement as 3- and 4-year-old children quickly seem to master the use of the device and its associated apps. Although young children's adeptness with computers has previously been recognised (Brooker & Siraj-Blatchford, 2002; Siraj-Blatchford & Whitebread, 2003), something different seems to be going on with the iPad and other tablet devices. The iPad is a very different kind of computer when compared with desktop and laptop computers of the very recent past. Young children seem to be able to interact with the tablet's touch-screen interface more easily than they can use a keyboard and mouse. The number of apps available on the iPad – including games and entertainment apps specifically designed for young children – far exceeds the software that was previously available to this age group. Unlike a desktop or even laptop computer, the iPad is lightweight and mobile and can be used in any part of the family home, in the car, while visiting friends or in any other space or place parents and caregivers choose to make it available to children. For young children, the iPad is more like an interactive toy than a computer.

Unlike most toys, though, iPads are a highly sophisticated 'convergence' technology (Jenkins, 2006) that combines multiple affordances that enable the individuals who interact with it, whether children or adults, to consume media, access information and communicate in multiple ways. The iPad converges the affordances of older media technologies like television, film, radio, music players and newspapers with new technologies like the internet and video games. It allows access to books, encyclopaedias, dictionaries and the collections of museums and archives. In addition, the device enables photography, video production, word processing, desktop publishing and audio recording and mixing, and provides the software to combine any or all of these. The iPad seems to be easy to use and yet allows access to vast information and rich participation in communications practices. If this was not enough, Apple's sophisticated marketing has established the iPad as an object of desire for many people, including children (Nielsen Newswire, 2012). It is not surprising many educators see great potential for the iPad to be used in classrooms. Around the post-industrialised world, iPads are being deployed by teachers in single classrooms, by principals across schools and by administrators across whole districts. This book is about the ways in which iPads are being used for developing literacy and creativity in three preschools in Brisbane, Australia. It outlines research we undertook during the course of a single year in partnership with the teachers, children, parents and caregivers in the preschools. We wanted to look past the hype associated with iPads to see what occurred when these devices were used with 3- and 4-year-old children.

Why iPads?

When we began our research project, the iPad was the principal tablet computer available in the marketplace, particularly within early years education settings. They were the logical choice of tablet for our project. As we write this book, the iPad and Apple's App Store is facing welcome competition from Android tablet devices and Google Play, including Google Play for Education and Microsoft's Surface tablets, which use the Windows operating system. We believe this competition is likely to be positive for the education sector as these large corporations compete with each other to seek market share through providing high-quality devices and software. We would particularly welcome improvements to the ways in which educational apps are provided and recommended through Apple's App Store. While it seems to be a strength that an enormous amount of software has been made available for the iPad for 3- and 4-year-old children, the trade-off is that it is difficult for teachers and parents to identify good-quality apps. As we will show in this book, it is unhelpful to try to identify the 'best apps' in a project like ours, as so much of the benefit of using particular apps comes from the curriculum development and pedagogy that exists around the app. There is no doubt, though, that the commercialisation of educational software through a semi-open marketplace like iTunes has significant implications for how iPads may be used in early years education. A concern we have about apps designed as 'educational software', particularly those created for young children, is that they often seem to promote a transmission model of learning in which it is assumed children will learn simply by interacting with an app. As we will consistently argue throughout this book, children most effectively learn with apps when they are involved in constructivist pedagogies. Furthermore, there is evidence that the design features of book apps may detract from attainment of literacy outcomes (Roskos *et al.*, 2012) and that 'no-cost' book apps, in particular, may be of lower quality than 'cost' book apps (Parette *et al.*, 2014).

We have no affiliation with Apple, or with the companies that produce the apps we discuss in this book, but we are highly aware that our project and this book have the potential to make us seem partisan and in favour of Apple products. We do believe it is important, though, to recognise the specificity of the affordances of the iPad or any other tablet device we may deploy in future research projects. Tablets are not all the same, nor do they function in exactly the same ways and this should be taken into account when we are trying to understand how children develop literacies and creativity using the devices. It is, therefore, important to name the device being used, rather than use a general descriptor like 'tablet' computer; hence our constant reference to the 'iPad' throughout this book. There is also a theoretical and cultural dimension to naming the iPad as the focus of our research. As du Gay *et al.* (1997) noted in their influential study of the Sony Walkman mobile music player, it is impossible to understand the device merely as a technology, it also has to be understood through the ways in which enters the 'circuit of culture' and becomes taken up through not only consumption, but production, representational processes, identity work and regulation.

Although our focus in this book is on the iPad's role in specific education settings, all of the dimensions outlined by du Gay and colleagues are accounted for as we recognise that education occurs in specific socio-material contexts and it matters that iPads were being deployed in the preschools rather than a different technological system. For instance, the children's desire to interact with the iPads cannot be separated from Apple's marketing of the product. The children's ability to produce their own media cannot be separated from the specific affordances of the iPad – its size and shape and the type of camera and apps it makes available. The ways in which individuals are provided with more or less control over how iPad use can be regulated through the 'parental controls' and functions like 'guided access' must be understood as part of Apple's response to its consumers' needs. More broadly, the iPad is not just a technology; it has staked a claim within the popular cultural experiences of many children and their adult teachers and parents and has entered public discourse about the role of technology in society and education. In this sense, the iPad has social and material specificity that must be accounted for as we aim to understand its use in education (see also, Rowsell, 2014).

The project

We undertook the research for this project in three preschools[1] located in Brisbane, Australia. The project was made possible through a partnership between QUT's Children and Youth Research Centre, The Gowrie – an organisation responsible for the management of 75 affiliated preschools and a grant through a philanthropic organisation, the Ian Potter Foundation. Each of the three preschools was located in either a low socio-economic or culturally diverse community. An important objective of the study was to explore ways to promote 'digital inclusion' through literacy and creativity for children and their families, at risk of being disadvantaged within digital culture and the digital economy. Internationally, digital inclusion has been identified as one of the keys to overall social inclusion and the development of digital literacy knowledge and skills are recognised as essential to digital inclusion (Williams, 2011).

As part of the Europe 2020 Initiative, the European Commission has identified 'Enhancing digital literacy, skills and inclusion' as one of the seven 'pillars' of the 'Digital Agenda for Europe' and education as a fundamental aspect of promoting digital inclusion (European Commission, 2014). In the United States, the Obama administration's 'ConnectED Initiative' recognises the need to promote digital literacy in both informal and formal learning environments, from K-12 (United States Government, 2013). In Australia, the Australian Curriculum, Assessment and Reporting Authority (ACARA) has included media arts, which has a strong focus on digital literacy, as a mandatory component of the Australian national arts curriculum, to be made available to all children from preschool to year six (ACARA, 2014). It is not obvious, however, what the development of digital literacies might 'look like' for preschool-aged children. An important objective of our project, therefore, was to explore digital literacies through the theoretical lenses available to the members of our team who work within print-based literacy, new literacies, digital media literacies and arts education. We wanted to apply nuanced understandings of digital literacy to our understandings of how young children learn through multimodal communication, storytelling and the creative representation of the world using digital technologies. A key goal was to explore the digital literacy knowledge and skills young children might develop in preschool to assist them to participate successfully in the first years of formal schooling. In this sense, we set out to explore what the new 'digital basics' might consist of and how the deployment of iPads could assist young children to develop these 'basics'. In the conclusion of the book, we will have more to say about what we think these 'basics' might consist of, as foundational experiences for the development of digital literacies. We do not put these 'basics' forward as a list of skills and knowledge to be 'ticked off', but present them as opportunities for young children to develop literacy and creativity.

To meet the project's objectives, ten iPads, iTunes credit and a laptop computer were purchased for each preschool for the teachers to use with the children to explore, play and learn. Parents and caregivers were invited to take part in workshops focused on using the iPads for literacy and creativity development and they were then able to borrow the iPads to take home for their children to use. The teachers took part in a series of professional development, planning and evaluation days on campus at the university and the teachers' commitment as co-investigators was integral to the implementation of the project. The teachers were asked to use the iPads as part of the children's curriculum experiences, to be integrated into teacher-directed and facilitated learning rather than as devices to use only during the children's free play sessions. This was considered important as previous research on the use of technology in early years centres shows that technology is sometimes provided as a free play option rather than as a directed learning experience for young children (Plowman & Stephen, 2005). The teachers had the autonomy to integrate the iPads in ways they judged to be appropriate, but were encouraged to explore different approaches and to take advantage of the different affordances of the iPads.

During professional development sessions, the teachers were introduced to a range of apps the university researchers believed worth trying out with the students. These included some apps designed specifically for young children's literacy development such as letter and number recognition games. A range of interactive books was introduced to the teachers for possible use with the children because the team wanted to explore different approaches to reading. Apps for creativity and storytelling were also made available and the teachers were shown how to use the iPads to draw, take photographs, record video and audio and then use apps to combine these digital materials into multimedia products. The intention was that the teachers would take these new resources and skills back to their preschools and investigate the possibilities. The research team was intent not to impose a specific set of activities or curriculum to be adhered to by the teachers as we wanted the implementation of the iPads to be as 'organic' as possible. As the project progressed and the teachers reported back on their reflections about the use of the iPads in their preschools, we found that they tended to challenge themselves to try out new pedagogical approaches and to use the iPads for different aspects of curriculum.

The preschools are geographically dispersed throughout Brisbane's suburbs and we have called them the 'Northern', 'Outer Northern' and 'Southern' preschools. The Northern preschool is located 20kms from Brisbane's central business district (CBD) and is surrounded by housing estates, mostly built since the 1980s. The Outer Northern preschool is located 45kms from Brisbane's CBD in a small satellite city that includes a mix of older and new, low-cost housing estates and semi-rural housing allotments. The Southern Preschool is located 15kms from Brisbane's CBD in an area that has developed from a small farming town in the mid-nineteenth century into the highly multicultural suburb that exists today. The suburb includes significant numbers of people born outside Australia, particularly from China, Taiwan, India and Vietnam.

We gathered data for the project through observations of the children using the iPads, interviews with teachers, parents/caregivers and children and through collecting student-produced artefacts, including photographs, art works, videos, iBooks and voice recordings. At the beginning of the project we asked the teachers and parents to complete surveys about their own use of digital technologies, their attitudes toward children using digital technologies and their opinions about the use of technologies in preschool spaces for education. During the professional development and evaluation days we audio-recorded key sessions where teachers were reflecting on the successes and challenges they were experiencing. At the end of the project, we also asked the teachers to complete an online questionnaire about their experiences during the project and to provide their recommendations for other teachers wanting to introduce iPads into preschools. In each chapter of the book we provide greater detail about how these data were analysed.

Our critical socio-material approach

Each of us brings different theoretical perspectives to this study but we broadly identify with critical socio-material approaches to understanding literacy and creativity. We believe this book's strength is that different theoretical lenses are used to make sense of children's play and learning with iPads. By 'critical', we mean an approach to research that is continually questioning and self-reflexive. Rather than setting out to prove a hypothesis or particular position in relation to children's use of iPads in preschools, we went into the project with open minds. As we implemented the project, collected data and analysed them, we tried to challenge our own assumptions, biases and positions. We were particularly aware of the need to avoid the assumption that iPads would necessarily improve children's learning or that children in this age group should or would be able to start developing digital literacies. We also wanted to avoid making assumptions about children's abilities to use the iPads – to either assume that they would be able to do particular things or that their age would necessarily limit what they could do. Of course, it is well established that it is not possible to step outside our own histories as researchers, but by attempting to be aware of these histories we have aimed to be open to a range of possibilities as we have read and interpreted our data.

The social part of our 'social-material' approaches refers to our common understanding that literacies are socially situated practices (Heath, 1983) and that meaning is generated in specific social and cultural contexts. Literacy is not a thing that is 'out there' to be acquired; rather literacies are enacted in everyday communications practices and literacy becomes normative through processes of institutionalisation. Likewise, culture and creativity occur in people's everyday practices (Williams, 1983; Willis, 1990). The institutionalisation of 'the Arts' through formal schooling and commercial and public institutions present specific instances of artist practice that generally have various forms of exchange value, whether this exists as economic, social or cultural capital (Bourdieu, 1979/2013). A social understanding of literacy and the arts helps us to understand young children's playful literate and creative practices as they begin to grapple with processes of normative literacy development and creative practice.

The 'material' in our 'socio-material' approach recognises that discursive accounts of literacy and creativity tell only part of the story of what it means to develop literacy and creativity (Clarke, 2002; Dezuanni & Woods, 2014; Fenwick & Edwards, 2010; Luke, 1992). The materiality of the body and the ways we become disciplined to interact with built spaces, technologies, furniture, books, cutlery, artistic materials and sports equipment – to name just a few things – is also central to how we develop literacy and creativity (Bourdieu, 1979/2013; Foucault, 1984; Latour, 2005/2007). Preschools are spaces in which children are invited to interact not just with other children and adults, but also indoor and outdoor areas and a large range of playthings, materials and equipment. iPads are 'material' and invite particular kinds of interactions that allow children to communicate and create. From this perspective, we believe it is important to recognise both the discursive and material ways in which children develop literacy and creativity.

The organisation of the book

We chose to write this book in teams of two as each of us has a history of involvement in research that provides us with particular theoretical and methodological perspectives to bring to bear on literacy and arts education. We wanted to recognise, though, that the arts and literacy are not separate domains and so our authoring 'pairs' combine knowledge from both fields. We also circulated the chapters among the whole team to get a range of insights, while respecting the specificity of the theories and methodologies of the authoring teams. Through this process, we have aimed to generate rich accounts of children's development of literacy and creativity with the iPads.

In Chapter 1 Dooley and Dezuanni look at the literate practices brought into being through iPad-embedded literacy education events. The authors describe literacy events involving the use of book apps, 'educational' apps and creating apps and device functions such as the camera. Through these events children learnt story literacy, scientific literacy and basic skills development. The authors locate this literacy learning within traditions of literacy education that were established during the print era and are being digitalised through platforms that include the iPad. They draw attention to pedagogic conundrums that arise as teachers take the iPad up within a broader context of curriculum and pedagogic reform.

In Chapter 2, Gattenhof and Dezuanni provide an overview of the role of mobile digital technologies in the lives of young children and the ways they were deployed in the preschools for arts-based learning activities. The chapter argues that mobile digital technologies are fast becoming ubiquitous in young children's homes and that this has implications for early years educational environments. For this reason, the chapter suggests arts education engagement in preschools should include the use of digital technologies. In the preschools in our study, the integration of the iPads into the children's arts experiences required careful curriculum planning and reflection on pedagogical practice to ensure the maintenance of a playful and discovery-based approach to teaching and learning in the arts. The chapter provides both a theoretical and contemporary curriculum perspective and is organised around three principles of best practice for iPad-based arts and creative education in early years centres.

The physicality of the iPad as an object, and how that might affect how children develop their drawing and writing skills is the focus of Chapter 3, led by Knight and Dooley. The authors ask how writing and drawing are done differently on the smooth glass surface of the iPad, compared to the ways children write and draw with physical tools and materials such as a pencil and paper. The authors argue the iPad is revolutionary in the way it fills a gap between the computer and the smartphone and that this uniqueness makes the iPad an object that can be easily adapted for use in preschools. This is not a simple adoption, however, as reflected in public discourse about the possible effects of the high-tech-cool iPad on natural, 'organic' childhoods. The authors' observations of how young children used iPads to write and draw in ways that differ to paper-based drawing and writing helped expose how these complexities play out on a micro scale. In these ways, the authors examine whether the materiality of the iPad affects children's early literacy experiences and how children write and draw, in relation to popular interest into the potential educational benefits for children's use of the technology.

In Chapter 4, Dezuanni and Gattenhof turn their attention to children's development of digital media literacies with iPads in preschool settings. Digital media literacies are located within the broader field of media education, which the authors show is necessary to ensure that 'digital literacy' is not defined as a narrow set of instrumental skills and practices. Since at least the 1930s, media education has been deployed as a protectionist response to concerns about children's interactions with media, with a focus on teaching children and young people to critically read media texts. The young children in our project participate in complex media ecologies, consuming and interacting with media across a variety of 'transmedia' experiences that call for new understanding of what it means to be 'media literate'. The chapter cites contemporary approaches to media education that promote reflective participation with digital culture, through both production and consumption, to argue the iPad provides preschool children with a resource for media production that enables them to develop digital media literacies. The chapter outlines a model for digital media literacies that includes the application of *digital materials* and *media concepts* through the processes of *media production* and *media analysis*. The model is then used as a framework to interpret children's media production work across the preschools in our project.

Chapter 5, led by Gattenhof and Dezuanni considers how the iPad and selected apps such as Puppet Pals, Popplet and Draw & Tell can assist children in participatory storying. The chapter focuses on re-telling and sequencing story moments that can assist young children in their acquisition of literacy and development of self-identity. The authors draw upon artefacts created by the preschool children, their teachers and their caregivers during the project to offer examples of practice for preschool teachers in supporting children in their recounting of real or imagined events using the iPad. The chapter also discusses possible approaches for engagement with the iPads that combine live and mediated representations of a story.

Chapter 6 examines visual arts learning and children's engagement with iPads. Knight and Dooley consider how popular beliefs about children's art tend to define what is considered 'authentic', how children's art is regarded, and also what forms it should typically take. The authors argue the dominance of developmental theories in early childhood education have effectively segmented children's art into schematic stages; these orderings closely intertwine children's art making with education agendas and show how child art is seen to primarily perform education-based tasks. The deep-seated and persistent fascination with why children make imagery means that children's art is rarely neutral but is often romanticised and constantly scanned for meaning. In education contexts where development discourses ground children's creative work with specific meanings, norms are established around what young children's art should look like. Crucially, this affects how arts activities are delivered to young children because educators often provide materials for making art products that they have already pictured in their minds. The authors argue that definitions of child art can be disrupted when preschool children use iPads to create visual work. Although child art discourses might affect how the art made on an iPad is regarded, introducing iPads provides exciting new ways for young children to make art.

In Chapter 7, Dooley and Gattenhof look at home-preschool relations around the iPad. They provide an account of the iPad loan programme by which participating children were able to take a project iPad home from their preschool centre, much as they would borrow books and puzzles. This component of the project was designed to assist parents to use the iPad at home to create rich storytimes with their children and to engage in playful and productive communicative activity. The loan programme is understood in the chapter as a family literacy initiative, that is, in relation to the ways literacy is used and learnt as part of everyday life in home and community. An epistemological analysis of three key issues is conducted: understandings of literacy, literacy goals, and literacy development and acquisition. This gives purchase on the epistemological tensions negotiated at both home and preschool in a broader educational environment where there is tension between the pursuit of print and digital basics. Implications are drawn for ongoing collaboration of home and preschool in working strategically together on this complex terrain.

In Chapter 8, Dezuanni and Knight explore the preschools as networked spaces into which the iPads were introduced, networks which involve the mediation of complex relationships between children and adults, physical and virtual technology and other materials like toys, play spaces, art materials and books. The chapter employs actor–network theory to explore negotiations between children, iPads, teachers and preschool spaces and materials, and aims to explain how these actors come to 'coexist' and lead to the development of literacy and creativity in specific ways. The authors explore the technological affordances of the iPad and the knowledge and skills children and teachers bring to interactions with the iPads to gain insight into how these various actors were able to enrol and mobilise each other. This approach particularly draws attention to specific challenges faced by the teachers as they negotiated a range of complex demands and obstacles to make the iPads available to the children for play and learning. It also highlights the need for new pedagogical approaches in preschools to enable the full potential of the iPads to be mobilised.

We have written this book as university-based researchers, but we hope it will be of use to readers outside academia. The insights we gained from working with three preschools as they immersed themselves in the use of iPads over the course of a year are well worth sharing with preschool teachers and parents, and educators more generally. We have attempted to get beyond the extremes of opinion that sometimes dominate popular discussions about young children's interactions with iPads and technology more generally: that iPads will either transform education in necessarily positive ways, or that they will lead to the ruination of childhood and education as we know it. As we argue in the following chapters, in many ways iPads *are* revolutionary, in the sense that they are a new type of technology available to young children. At the same time, the ways in which they can become part of the development of literacy and creativity are highly contingent on many factors, including the need to transform pedagogy and curriculum design. Our work also has implications for policy makers, particularly with respect to the ways in which teachers are supported through access to professional development and technical advice and assistance to manage complex technological systems. We see this book as a contribution to broader critical discussions about the educational uses of iPads, particularly in the literacy and arts education fields, and we hope readers will find it useful for their own considerations of technology in education.

Note

1 These preschools are actually called 'community kindergartens' in Brisbane. Kindergarten is a commonly used name in Queensland for education programs provided for 3- and 4-year-old children, although the term 'preschool' is also sometimes used. Preschool is often used in other Australian States. In the United Kingdom, a common name is 'nursery school' while in the United States and several other countries 'preschool' is commonly used. We chose to use 'preschool' throughout this book as the most commonly used international description.

References

ACARA (2014). The Australian Curriculum, the Arts. www.australiancurriculum.edu.au/TheArts Accessed June 27, 2014.

Bourdieu, P. (1979/2013). *Distinction: A social critique of the judgement of taste.* New York: Routledge.

Brooker, L. & Siraj-Blatchford, J. (2002). 'Click on Miaow!': How children of three and four years experience the nursery computer. *Contemporary Issues in Early Childhood*, 3(2), 251–73.

Clarke, J. (2002). A new kind of symmetry: Actor–network theories and the new literacy studies. *Studies in the Education of Adults*, 34(2), 107–22.

Dezuanni, M.L. & Woods, A.F. (2014). Developing media production skills for literacy in a primary school classroom: digital materials, embodied knowledge and material contexts. In Georgina Barton (ed.), *Literacy in the Arts: Retheorising learning and teaching* (pp. 143–60). Springer International Publishing, Switzerland.

du Gay, P., Hall, S., Janes, L., Madsen, A.K., Mackay, H. & Negus, K. (1997). *Doing Cultural Studies: The story of the Sony Walkman*. London: SAGE Publications.

European Commission (2014). Pillar VI: Enhancing digital literacy, skills and inclusion. http://ec.europa.eu/digital-agenda/en/our-goals/pillar-vi-enhancing-digital-literacy-skills-and-inclusion. Accessed June 28, 2014.

Fenwick, T. & Edwards, R. (2010). *Actor–network Theory in Education*. London: Routledge.

Foucault, M. (1984). The means of correct training. In P. Rabinow (ed.), *The Foucault Reader*. London: Penguin Books.

Heath, S.B. (1983). *Ways with Words: Language, life, and work in communities and classrooms*. New York and Cambridge: Cambridge University Press.

Jenkins, H. (2006). *Convergence Culture: Where old and new media collide*. New York: New York University Press.

Latour, B. (2005/2007). *Reassembling the Social: An introduction to actor–network theory*. Oxford: Oxford University Press.

Luke, A. (1992). The body literate: discourse and inscription in early literacy training. *Linguistics and Education*, 4, 107–29.

Nielsen Newswire (2012, November 20). U.S. kids continue to look forward to 'IHOLIDAY'. www.nielsen.com/us/en/newswire/2012/u-s-kids-continue-to-look-forward-to-iholiday.html Accessed June 27, 2014.

Parette, H.P., Blum, C. & Luthin, K. (2014). A quantitative features analysis of recommended no- and low-cost preschool e-books. *Early Childhood Education Journal*, DOI: 10.1007/s10643-013-0611-8

Plowman, L. & Stephen, C. (2005). Children, play, and computers in preschool education. *British Journal of Educational Technology*, 36(2), 145–57.

Roskos, K., Burstein, K., You, B.K., Brueck, J. & O'Brien, C. (2012). A formative study of an e-book instructional model in early literacy. *Creative Education*, 2(1), 10–17.

Rowsell, J. (2014). Toward a phenomenology of contemporary reading. *Australian Journal of Language and Literacy*, 37(2), 117–27.

Siraj-Blatchford, J. & Whitebread, D. (2003). *Supporting ICT in the Early Years*. Berkshire: McGraw-Hill Education.

United States Government (2013). ConnectED Initiative. www.whitehouse.gov/issues/education/k-12/connected Accessed June 28, 2014.

Williams, R. (1983). *Culture and Society: 1780–1950*. New York: Columbia University Press.

Williams, T. (2011). A fair go for all in the digital era: Towards a digital inclusion roadmap. Appendix 2, Digital Inclusion Summit Report. Huawei. www.rtirc.gov.au/files/2011/12/Huawei-Appendix-2-Digital-Inclusion-Summit-Report.pdf Accessed June 27, 2014.

Willis, P. (1990). *Common Culture: Symbolic work at play in the everyday cultures of the young*. Milton Keyes: Open University Press.

Chapter 1

Literacy and digital culture in the early years

Karen Dooley and Michael Dezuanni

Introduction

Guidelines for using the iPad for literacy education began appearing soon after the release of the device. They advise early years teachers about selecting book apps (e.g. Cahill & McGill-Franzen, 2013; Morgan, 2013; Zipke, 2013) and incorporating them into shared reading (Hoffman & Paciga, 2013), embedding educational apps into instructional routines for phonics and fluency (Northrop & Killeen, 2013; Reutschlin Schugar *et al.*, 2013; Thoermer & Williams, 2012), and using drawing, mind-mapping and other open-ended apps to teach comprehension strategies (Hutchison *et al.*, 2012). There is an air of excitement in this professional literature: mobile devices have been hailed as 'revolutionary' because they create 'opportunities to apply proven practices (the best ones) more often with all students' (Roskos & Neumann, 2014, p. 509). In short, the iPad is rich in possibilities for best practice.

But some question what has been described as the 'domestication' of the iPad to established forms of literacy education (O'Mara & Laidlaw, 2011). Literate practice on digital platforms, they argue, is more likely to require creative decision-making about multiple modes and tools than is print-based practice. It may entail considerably more author-audience collaboration because of the easy interconnectivity of both parties on social media platforms. Moreover, this flows through into learning, favouring collaborative relationships such as mentoring rather than the hierarchical transmissive relationships that seem to have a place in at least some aspects of print-based literacy education (Luke, 2008; Marsh & Yamada-Rice, 2013). Developed for print platforms, established practices of literacy education have yet to address these epistemic and pedagogic developments adequately. This has borne on the ways that the iPad is taken up in schools (Lynch & Redpath, 2014; O'Mara & Laidlaw, 2011).

Our aim here is to contribute to the normative conversation about the use of the iPad for literacy education. To this end, we look at iPad-based digitalisation of traditions of literacy education. Four broad traditions have been identified: the authentic, the didactic, the critical and the functional (Kalantzis & Cope, 2012). Each tradition is epistemically distinct, characterised by a particular way of making knowledge (Kalantzis & Cope, 2012; New London Group, 1996). The authentic tradition entails situated practice or experience of the known and the new. An example is the reading workshop approach in which children read and respond to literature with the support of mini-lessons as required (e.g. Serafini & Youngs, 2013). The didactic tradition entails overt instruction or conceptualising by naming and theorising. Synthetic phonics, the systematic and decontextualised teaching of sound-symbol relationships, is an example of this tradition (e.g. Lloyd, 1992). The critical tradition entails critical framing or analysing functionally. This tradition is exemplified by critical literacy approaches which enable children to examine contrasting versions of a story (e.g. Exley *et al.*, 2014). The functional tradition entails transformed practice or applying appropriately and creatively. An example is the genre approach to writing which develops children's awareness of the purpose of a genre such as narrative and the structure and language features of texts in that genre (e.g. Woods *et al.*, 2014).

Digitalisation of literacy education has long been envisaged (e.g. New London Group, 1996), although progress in the early years has been patchy, especially at the preschool level (Paciga *et al.*, 2013). Given this history, it is significant, then, that the advent of the iPad seems to have generated new digital possibilities – and enthusiasm. A recent review of research on touch-screen tablets and emergent literacy described what can be understood as experiential and didactic uses of book apps and 'educational' apps, presenting evidence of the efficacy of these (Neumann & Neumann, 2013). Preschool teacher uptake of such possibilities warrants investigation. Much of the contention around the embedding of the iPad into literacy education in the compulsory early years is paradigmatic and explained in terms of the institutionalisation of print-based norms in an era of curricular conservatism (Lynch & Redpath, 2014). But what of the pre-compulsory years?

Here we look at the uptake of the iPad in preschool from a perspective that assumes the epistemic moves of the traditions of literacy education are neither stages in some pedagogic formula nor in need of the 'balancing' so often touted as the solution to paradigmatic tension. Rather, they should be selected according to the learning goals for particular groups of students in a given context (Kalantzis & Cope, 2012). But what should those goals be? In this chapter we seek to inform this normative decision-making by describing and explaining the way contending paradigms are negotiated in the classroom as iPads are embedded in preschool literacy education.

We develop the chapter in three sections. First, we elaborate our analytic framework, introducing the concepts of literacy event and literate practice and specifying these for the iPad platform. Second, we present analyses of literacy activities that involved stories, scientific information, and basic skills, highlighting complications that arose in the enactment of one or another tradition of literacy education. Third, we return to normative conversation about the use of iPads for literacy education. We discuss paradigmatic conundrums related to the scarce classroom resource of adult time, suggesting some ways of thinking about these when planning literacy education in the early years.

iPad-embedded literacy education

To describe and explain iPad-embedded literacy education, we make use of the concepts of 'literacy event' and 'literate practice'. These concepts were developed originally for print-based literacy. The concept of 'literacy event' referred to:

> occasions in which written language is integral to the nature of participants' interactions and their interpretive processes and strategies. Familiar literacy events for mainstream pre-schoolers are bedtime stories, reading cereal boxes, stop signs . . . In such literacy events, participants follow socially established rules for verbalizing what they know from and about the written material. Each community has rules for socially interacting and sharing knowledge in literacy events.
>
> (Heath, 1982, p. 50)

Literate practice referred originally to the social practices brought into being through the print-based literacy events of a given community, along with the conceptions of reading and writing inherent in these (Street, 1984, p. 1). It drew attention to the particularity of the ways literacy is used in a given context for specific purposes and to attendant relations of power. Three decades on, this concept, along with that of literacy event, has been extended beyond the written language of print texts to visual and other modes integral to literacy on digital platforms (e.g. Marsh, 2005; Pahl & Rowsell, 2005; Street, 1997, 2009). To describe textual modes in iPad-embedded literacy events, we use a version of the typology suggested originally by the New London Group (1996).

The multiliteracies manifesto (New London Group, 1996) called for instruction in five modes additional to the linguistic. These were the audio, the spatial, the gestural and the visual – and in the case of digital multimedia texts, the multimodal. The manifesto was re-visited a decade or so later by some of its authors (Cope & Kalantzis, 2009). At that time it was argued that multimodality was more central than it had been in the mid-1990s (Cope & Kalantzis, 2009). Written language, it was noted, was increasingly coupled with the visual, not only in digital texts such as blogs and email, but also in textbooks, magazines, newspapers and other print forms influenced by digital conventions. At the same time, greater delicacy was achieved by splitting the linguistic mode into the written and the oral, and adding a new mode: the tactile.

We make use of the revised list of modes (Cope & Kalantzis, 2009). The distinction between the written and the oral is especially useful for analysing data produced with young children. In the early years, the oral is taught as both a mode in its own right and as a means of access to the written mode. With respect to the tactile, however, we found the notion of touch as 'means of activation' of texts (Bezemer & Kress, 2014) to be useful. In other words, we do not treat the tactile as a mode – a set of conventional communication resources – although there are conditions under which that would be appropriate (Bezemer & Kress, 2014; Walsh & Simpson, 2014).

Recent research has complemented the concept of mode with that of interactivity (Rowsell, 2014). Critics have argued that understandings of literacy need to go beyond modal design to the embodied experience of literacy as creative play (Jacobs, 2014; Leander & Boldt, 2013). Consistent with this, a phenomenological perspective on reading (Rowsell, 2014) has shown how iPads enable a continuum of interactive reading experience. The eBook is located at the end of the continuum where reading experience is most similar to that of print reading; video games are at the other end. In between, in order of increasing interactivity, are websites, multimodal iBooks and social media. Similarly, recent research has brought the creative play involved in writing to the fore (Dezuanni & Woods, 2014).

In summary, we draw on an expanded typology of touch-activated modes (Kalantzis & Cope, 2012), a continuum of interactivity (Rowsell, 2014), and understandings of writing as creative play (Dezuanni & Woods, 2014) to specify the concept of literacy events (Heath, 1982) for iPad-embedded literacy activity. We now present analyses conducted within this framework, looking in turn at literacy events built around stories, scientific information and basic skills. In doing so, we consider the traditions of literacy education (Kalantzis & Cope, 2012) in which these literacy events are rooted and the literate practices (Street, 1984) they bring into being.

The research evidence

Stories

Book apps were integral to some story-based literacy events at all three study sites. The stories on these apps can be understood as 'iBooks', that is, as touch-activated multimodal narratives (Rowsell, 2014). Unlike the eBook, the iBook integrates multiple semiotic modes, typically, the written, oral, visual and audio. Yet, unlike the video game, it has a linear narrative that exercises control over the reader's meaning-making processes. In addition, book apps used in our study included activities such as manipulating images or colouring in. We now look in detail at story-based iBook reading events in one of the three centres. These data are presented here because they offer insights into some forms of literacy education common in early years classrooms; they are not meant to be representative of the study sites.

iBook re-reading

In interviews conducted over the course of the study year, the focal teacher described her ideal iBook reading event: a small group activity initiated by children during free play and enacted without adult participation. The story viewed or 'read' by the children is one with which they are familiar from whole-class storytime. In one variant, several children sit around a single iPad 'peer tutoring and chatting'; in another, they use the same app, but on individual iPads, talking with each other while listening to the story at their own pace through headphones or doing some of the non-reading activities on the app. In either case, the children are persistent; they do not skip from app to app.

The teacher's ideal iBook reading event was established in the focal classroom three terms into the preschool year. iBooks had been available from the beginning of the year, but had been little used. In the fifth month of the study, the teacher observed that the children 'haven't used the stories a lot'. If the children did open book apps at that time, they did not persist with the whole story. This was a point of contrast with the use of phonics and other educational apps the children viewed as 'games'. To redress the lack of interest in book apps, the teacher loaded iBook versions of familiar print books onto iPads that she then put into the story corner. By way of interpretative background, it should be noted that print books and iBooks had been available in learning areas around the room since the beginning of the year; stories had never been confined to story corner.

> [I was] trying to get them to use the iPad for reading stories; they weren't reading stories on it anywhere [in the room]. So we figured if we start there [in story corner], where they know, then they'll know what stories are on there. They were skipping over the stories and going for the gamey things.

The teacher encouraged children to use the iBooks during free play time, providing 'direct teaching' as required to enable operation of the device and apps. She also encouraged exploration of the 'extras', for example, colouring in, manipulation of images, and sign and foreign language options. By the fourth term, the teacher was able to withdraw from iBook reading events because the children were motivated and skilled enough for a 'free access' approach to be successful. In the final term of the study, children chose to 'revisit and revisit and revisit stories that they . . . [were] familiar with'. The child-centredness evident here was not limited to iBook reading events. Generally, learning in the focal classroom turned on child motivation and interest; the teacher's role was facilitative, although she made some strategic use of direct instruction.

For the focal teacher, part of the attraction of the iPad lay in the opportunity for revisiting stories during free play. The teacher said that the combination of whole-class storytime with repeated individual and small group iBook reading seemed to have improved the quality of children's stories and their oral language:

> I think their stories that they have come up with and their oral language, because we've used a combination, is better this year than it has been in previous years. Because I think they went back themselves to reading that story or hearing that story over and over of *Goldilocks and the Three Bears.*

In the past, the teacher herself had read books repeatedly to children during free play. But she thought children were now less motivated and interested in book reading: 'not as much in their free play time do we have children saying, "Will you read this to me?" They don't come and ask you anymore'. The teacher said that she now had to initiate the activity but the number of children with special needs now attending preschool meant she had little time to do so. When one of us recalled revisiting books with individuals and small groups virtually every day of the preschool year, the teacher re-iterated: 'I'd be lucky to do that every week; we'd be lucky to do that even sometimes once a month'. Instead, the teacher tried to enlist parental support in the classroom and to encourage parents to read more to their children at home. Repeated reading on the iPad helped also: 'to . . . get that literacy happening in the technology is filling a bit of that deficit that's been there'.

In the focal classroom, the reading of book apps was linked with storytime, a whole-class, print book, read aloud activity. During storytime the teacher provided an animated reading of a print book, inviting children to join in where possible from the illustrations and memory of past readings. The teacher also led discussions to develop the children's knowledge of the technology of the book (e.g. 'cover', 'title') and comprehension of a given story. In one of her interviews, she gave examples of questions asked to those ends: 'What was the sequence? Who was the character? What happened before? What happened next?'

Several activities other than repeated iBook reading were either part of storytime or linked to it. These included story re-tellings and dramatisations, text innovation and music activities. We now look at how the iPad was used for two of these activities: story re-telling and text innovation.

Multimodal story re-telling

In her final interview 11 months into the project, the teacher mentioned a multimodal re-telling of *Goldilocks and the Three Bears.* She had experimented with this activity during the study and intended to extend it to more children in 2014.

> We only did that [re-telling] with two [children]. They all had the story at group time and we all did activities and things around Goldilocks and we role-played and dramatized and did music. But then, a couple of the children, [research assistant] did one and I did one, we used the little tiny

> bears that I had and then we used equipment from within the room to retell the story, set it up, take the photos and then retell the story. [Child's] was brilliant. I was just listening to it the other day. It's absolutely fantastic, the verbal language that he was able to recall and the storyline and the extra bits that he put in and the extension of his vocabulary, it was just amazing, just amazing.

A book-making app was used for the story re-telling activity. This type of app has been described as a 'creating app' for it enables construction of a range of texts (Neumann & Neumann, 2013). In this case, the teacher mentored the child in creative decisions about still images and monologue. While expected to work with the storyline and language of the original print book, the child could add 'extra bits'. The number of participants in this creative multimodal literacy event was notably small: there were two adult–child dyads. The reason for this was that the children required intensive support to begin, develop and complete the re-telling. Ten months into the study, the teacher emphasised that this type of literacy event was most demanding of her time:

> [apps which] require adults to help with the photography or with making a story or making suggestions, they just flick through from one to another . . . to actually start something, and finish it, needs an adult support.

The teacher thought that there was an absolute limit of about four on the number of children who could be involved in such a literacy event at any one time. She said that a pedagogy different from hers might increase that number. However, she was not in favour of that, even in the year of compulsory schooling that followed the preschool year:

> in a more structured environment with direct teaching, it may be [possible to have more children working on those literacy activities], you know, though I would like to see . . . [the first year of school] not have any more structure than it's already got.

The teacher was speaking of an environment in which children have less control of their learning than in preschool. She was not averse to direct instruction per se; indeed, she took that option up to enable iBook reading, instructing children directly in hardware and software operation, although not in literacy content. Like many in the sector, the teacher was wary of the creeping didacticism of early years pedagogy. By way of background, it should be noted that the study was conducted at a time of some pedagogic anxiety. Play-based learning has long been dominant locally (Chiang, 2010). But among preschool teachers there is concern that the introduction of a compulsory year of schooling for 4½–5½-year-olds in the state, and the implementation of Australia's first national curriculum in that year, has ushered in more prescriptive curriculum and more teacher-directed instruction. In the year preceding the study, one of us encountered this position repeatedly in early years professional development forums. At the preschool level it took the form of concern about what the focal teacher described as the 'pushdown' of pedagogic settings from the compulsory years.

iBook text innovation

The focal teacher's pedagogic position is evident also in her account of a text innovation literacy event. During the project planning meeting in the tenth month of the study, the teacher described her efforts to introduce this activity. She said that she had begun with a print version of a book with a repetitive story structure and rhythmic sentence structure: *Brown Bear, Brown Bear What Do You See?* To encourage text innovation, she had tried lines such as 'Panda, Panda, what do you see?' and '[Child's name, Child's name], what do you see?' Initially, she was able to recruit only one child to the activity. However, she had more success when she approached three girls who were playing in the preschool fairy garden and suggested, 'How about we get the iPad and video what you're doing and make a book about it?' Once again, the teacher was trying to spark child interest and motivation; she did not prescribe the activity. After recruiting the three girls, the teacher went on to help them make an iBook that required creative decisions about visual, written and oral modes in the form of moving images, writing and narration. Reflecting on the activity, the teacher was pleased that the girls had read their iBook repeatedly during the final months of the year. Once again, however, she raised the issue of time, 'they like to go back over it, but it took a lot of time'. And once again, she planned to manage this problem in 2014 by seeking more parent support in the classroom.

Story literacy

We have looked here at three iPad-embedded literacy events that were linked to whole group storytime in the focal classroom: iBook reading, multimodal story re-telling and iBook text innovation. These literacy events are part of a cluster that brings into being what the focal teacher described as 'story literacy', a form of schooled literate practice in which reading and writing are conceived of as processes of narrative meaning-making. This practice was taught through a version of shared book reading. As first described four decades ago (Holdaway, 1979), the shared book approach begins with animated whole-class read-alouds. Children are then moved toward independent experience and expression through activities that include discussion of the story; repeated readings; re-tellings; and text innovation. To enable repeated readings, teachers were originally urged to embrace the technology of the 'listening post' – a learning station equipped with a tape recorder, a print book, and a tape of the story:

> We gain much greater control over repetitions when we bring a listening post into the room. The less ready children are then able to gain much more massive repetition before 'reading' than they otherwise would. The tape recorder seems to be the most important invention for literacy after the book.
>
> (Holdaway, 1979, p. 73)

The shared book approach has roots in the authentic tradition of literacy education (Kalantzis & Cope, 2012). The epistemic moves are experiential: children bring their meaning-making resources to text reception and production; teachers facilitate child activity; learning turns on child motivation and interest. In the focal classroom, the print book remained at the heart of this authentic form of literacy education but there was some digitalisation through iPad-embedded activities:

> I try to make sure the stories I have on there [the iPad], also, I have in hard copy too. Because I think that they need to know what a book is and how precious a book is. And we have the book, the fact that, yes, this is the book. But we can also have the book here [on the iPad] and what else can we do with the story that we now know? So the book has precedence in place over the story on the iPad.

As we have shown, repeated iBook reading was one of the things the children in the focal classroom could 'do with the story' they knew from the print book. The teacher valued this activity because it redressed what she saw as a limitation of the classroom programme that she attributed to the scarcity of teacher time. Effectively a digitalisation of the listening post, repeated iBook reading has been recommended to literacy educators (Thoermer & Williams, 2012). However, it has also been singled out as an activity that subordinates the iPad to print-based literacy education (Lynch & Redpath, 2014). But there was more to the teacher's shared book approach than print book read-alouds and an iPad-based listening post: the story re-telling and text innovation activities in the cluster of shared book literacy events provided opportunities for creative, multimodal decision-making on the iPad platform. The focal teacher was enthusiastic about her forays into this type of activity with one or two children. However, the authentic pedagogic settings of the classroom and the relative scarcity of adult time meant that the activity was limited to a few children in the class. For this teacher, the solution was to increase the amount of adult time available in the classroom, rather than to extend didacticism beyond software and hardware operation to literacy content. The same pedagogic issues arose in relation to iPad-embedded scientific literacy.

Scientific information

Websites and a creating app were integral to some science practices in the focal classroom; the websites were used for reading about scientific topics and the creating app for producing scientific texts. Websites provide opportunities for reading or viewing texts in multiple modes, most commonly the visual and the written, but sometimes also the oral, audio and multimodal. With respect to interactivity, the experience of reading a website tends to fall between that of the monomodal eBook and that of the multimodal iBook (Rowsell, 2014). Creating apps, we noted earlier, present relatively open-ended opportunities for text construction, sometimes in multiple modes. In what follows, we look first at a literacy event that involved website reading and then at one involving productive use of a creating app.

When interviewed during the eleventh month of the study, the focal teacher spoke enthusiastically of the iPad giving her 'the ability to research outside of books' with the children. Indeed, the teacher favoured iPad-embedded internet searches for scientific information over their print-based equivalent:

> We always talk to them [the children], when we want to know something . . . 'Let's look it up. How are we going to find that information out?' For example, an ant's body parts . . . It gives us that ability to look it up straight away, which has been great, but, we always looked it up straight away, but it's been in a book, we might not be able to find it . . . [I value] that ability to research and do things straight away . . . if we're out there [in the preschool yard], I can say, 'Go inside and get an iPad . . . and we'll look it up straight away'.

The literacy event described here includes at least one adult and any number of children. The event unfolds as the adult encourages and then leads an internet search on the iPad for information to answer questions that have come up in discussion. The literate practice is a schooled scientific one, dedicated to retrieving scientifically accurate information; the literacy education approach is authentic, turning on child interest. Websites are favoured because information searches are more convenient and success is more assured than with print books. In scientific literacy in this classroom, then, the print text does not enjoy the 'precedence' it has in story literacy.

An authentic approach is evident also in a poster-making activity observed by one of us during the ninth month of the project. Some of the data relating to this activity have been analysed in Chapter 2, highlighting the interactional work of adult and child. Here we consider that work as part of a literacy event. At the time of the poster-making activity, the class was raising a brood of chickens they had hatched in an incubator. A chicken theme was in progress. Among other things, the children had used the iPad to capture images of the chickens. The poster-making activity began with the project research assistant

Figure 1.1 Poster created using Comic Life

Source: plasq.com

Reprinted by permission of Plasq and children's parents

suggesting to the children that they might like to make a chicken poster on the iPad. It was at this point that our observation began.

During free play time the research assistant takes several children, each with an iPad, over to the chicken incubator where they capture some images. She then takes them back to a table where she shows them how to import still images into the Comic Life poster-making app. After that, she types in captions dictated by the children.

In this literacy event there is one adult participant and several children. The event unfolds with the adult suggesting and scaffolding the use of an unfamiliar creating app. The children exercise considerable control of their activity; they are free to join or leave and to take up the adult's suggestions as they wish. In an informal audio-recorded discussion at the end of the day, the research assistant said she had decided to 'see if some kids wanted to do something on the iPad about the chickens'. She 'knew that they hadn't used Comic Life before' and 'thought maybe we could learn a new program and use what they'd already been doing in class'. As shown in Chapter 2, her role was more facilitative than directive. Nonetheless, a constant adult presence was required:

> I sort of suggested things we could take photos of but I didn't actually say you should take a photo of this or I didn't really help them with the framing of the photos . . . some of the photos are actually really well framed so I didn't actually have to . . . I showed them how to use Comic Life and showed them how to add some photos that they took on their own . . . then I explained that we could add some words then and so the students told me what they wanted to put . . . and I then typed . . . you're always going to need that adult support to actually get those sentences into the program.

Like the story re-tellings and the text innovations, the poster-making provided opportunities for creative multimodal practice. It is notable, though, that this was enabled by the availability of an extra adult skilled in the mentoring approach favoured by the focal teacher and that it drew on photography skills already taught by the teacher the previous term, as described in Chapter 4. Indeed, one child who decided to join the activity when the researcher and the children had already begun putting posters together went to the incubator on her own and captured some images for her poster. Nonetheless, the research assistant spent most of the free play session working with the small poster-making group while the teacher and the teacher aide monitored and worked with the rest of the class.

The key point we are making here is that digitalised text production in the authentic tradition draws heavily on the scarce resource of adult time. This time pressure was less marked with didactic uses of the iPad, to which we now turn.

Figure 1.2 Photographing the chickens
Reprinted by permission of child's parents

Basic skills

'Educational apps' (hereafter, 'literacy apps') were integral to instruction in the written mode in all the study centres. These apps have been described as 'gaming apps' (Neumann & Neumann, 2013) because they have some of the characteristics of computer games. They are quite interactive, easily learnt, and offer extrinsic rewards in the form of points, certificates, stars and so forth; moreover, like games, they may be levelled so that challenge increases with demonstrated player skill. These are all features that compel mastery and motivation (Neumann & Neumann, 2013); indeed, as already noted, the children in the focal class 'were skipping over the stories and going for the gamey things' during free play. The teacher reported further that the children 'seem to like' phonics apps, sharing their achievements excitedly: 'I got all the levels'.

From early on, literacy apps such as Reading Eggs and Alpha Tots were available as a free play option in the focal classroom. Every time we visited, children were using these apps, generally with an adult or alone. The following observation is indicative. It shows what the rest of the class was doing while a few children were making the chicken posters.

> In learning areas around the room, some children are working with traditional art materials or chicken-themed manipulatives and books, while

> others are viewing nursery rhyme apps or working through counting and alphabet apps. The teacher aide is monitoring children in the learning areas. She goes over to a child using an alphabet app and encourages him to persist until he has finished the task he started.

When the iPads were first introduced, adults sat with the children, assisting them to operate the device, use the app, and understand the literacy content. As the year progressed, the children were observed working with less adult support. Time was a consideration, though. According to the focal teacher, 'the gamey things' were learnt more quickly than book apps and book creation apps but took longer, nonetheless, than 'the creative arts ones . . . the drawing'. In 2014 the teacher planned to enlist parent support to teach the literacy apps.

Basic knowledge of the written mode and skill in using it are potentially part of any number of literate practices. When taught through literacy apps, the didactic tradition is invoked to resource this potential. The epistemic moves of this tradition are conceptual, involving either memorisation or the learning of rules about the facts of the written mode (Kalantzis & Cope, 2012). Although digitalised by literacy apps, these are not the moves privileged on digital platforms (Marsh & Yamada-Rice, 2013). It is for this reason that the use of literacy apps recommended in the professional literature (Northrop & Killeen, 2013; Schugar, Smith & Schugar, 2013; Thoermer & Williams, 2012) has drawn criticism from some literacy educators (Lynch & Redpath, 2014; O'Mara & Laidlaw, 2011).

Didacticism is only one means of learning the written mode. At least some children catch on to reading through authentic literacy activities. There was some evidence of this happening with iPad-embedded iBook reading in the focal classroom. In the ninth month of the study one of the parents stated:

> He has also just started to read the iBooks on the . . . iPad and his favourite is *Goldilocks and the Three Bears*. He can read the story along with the narrator now and is starting to recognise some small words.

Moreover, scaffolding also has some place in authentic literacy education. Consider phonics: if children have not 'caught on to the idea' after letter–sound associations have been pointed out to them, then the teacher is encouraged to draw attention to some examples in familiar books and to get the children to spot them in new stories (Holdaway, 1979, p. 74). The point is that phonics has been taught – differently – from within both the authentic and didactic traditions. After some decades of prominence, the authentic tradition fell from favour during the late twentieth century. The 1990s and early 2000s saw an international push for a new didacticism bolstered by emerging psycholinguistic understandings of the reading process. As a consequence, synthetic phonics programs have been taken up in preschools where the analytic phonics of the authentic tradition was once dominant (Campbell *et al.*, 2011, 2014). In this context, the iPad enabled a digitalisation of this new didacticism in the focal classroom – teacher pedagogic inclination and time constraints notwithstanding.

Discussion and conclusions

The data we have presented here do not represent all the iPad-embedded literacy events and literate practices of the focal classroom, let alone the three preschools. Rather, they highlight pedagogic conundrums that may attend the introduction of the iPad into literacy education in the pre-compulsory preschool years. Specifically, the data show some digitalisation of the authentic tradition of education in both story and scientific literacies. The iPad was used as a digital listening post for stories and a platform for creating multimodal stories; it was used also for reading scientific websites and creating a multimodal science poster. The teacher's commitment to authentic literacy education meant that some of the epistemic moves and collaborative learning norms privileged in digital worlds were enacted in the focal classroom. However, without the infusion of additional resources of adult time, these did not seem scalable within that paradigm.

Our finding is not surprising. As was established long ago by the British sociologist Basil Bernstein (1975/2003), authentic instruction tends to be an expensive pedagogy reliant on an abundance of teacher time. Further, a recent study in a fifth grade classroom (Simpson & Walsh, 2014) has shown that the iPad can be particularly demanding of teacher time in less structured pedagogic moments because there are more tools and modes for children to explore on the iPad than on print-based platforms. As a result, teacher time is at a premium when creative play is meant to generate a product valued in school, for example, a story re-telling, a text innovation, a scientific poster or a persuasive advertisement. The fifth grade teacher managed this by ramping up whole-class, teacher-directed instruction in order to manage otherwise impossible time demands during the less structured moments of a unit on persuasive writing. Given the place of teacher-directed instruction in the functional tradition of genre pedagogy, this solution was paradigmatically palatable in a way that it was not in the focal classroom.

The digital time squeeze seemed to be most acute when authentic text production activities were enacted in the focal classroom, although the time demands of authentic text reception and didactic skills activities were not inconsiderable. As we have indicated, the teacher had a plan for managing these demands in future. She intended to bring parents into the classroom to increase the resources of adult time available to the children during free play. This might not be possible in all settings; moreover, normative questions remain. What should the goals of iPad-embedded literacy instruction be in a time-enriched classroom? What is the most productive use of both teacher and parent time? What our research suggests is the need for systematic planning of time resources informed by reflection on the particularities of iPad-embedded instruction in a given setting and with cognisance of paradigmatic options. To this end, we conclude by suggesting a set of reflective questions to inform this normative decision-making by teachers – the iPad-embedded Literacy Education Time Allocation Tool (iLETA Tool).

iPad-embedded Literacy Education Time Allocation Tool

How might this literacy event contribute to development of the epistemic moves and learning approaches appropriate to print- and/or digital-based literacies?

What prior knowledge and skill do children bring to this literacy event (hardware operation, software operation, literacy content)?

What is the learning priority? Is it to become more proficient at hardware and software operation or to build literacy content? Is it some combination of these?

What is my pedagogic preference? How will it contribute to attainment of the learning outcome? Would a different pedagogic tradition offer a more effective or feasible approach?

Who should support the children in the literacy event? Should it be me or the teacher aide? Should it be a parent? Who is best positioned to promote the outcome? What are the opportunity costs when the support role falls to me, the teacher aide or parents?

References

Bernstein, B. (1975/2003). *Towards a Theory of Educational Transmission. Class, codes and control (Vol III)*. London: Routledge.

Bezemer, J. & Kress, G. (2014). Touch: A resource for making meaning. *Australian Journal of Language and Literacy*, 37(2), 77–85.

Cahill, M. & McGill-Franzen, A. (2013). Selecting 'app'ealing and 'app'ropriate book apps for beginning readers. *The Reading Teacher*, 67(1), 30–9.

Campbell, S., Torr, J. & Cologon, K. (2011). Ants, apples and the ABCs: The use of commercial phonics programmes in prior-to-school children's services. *Journal of Early Childhood Literacy*, 12(4), 367–88.

—— (2014). Pre-packaging preschool literacy: what drives early childhood teachers to use commercially produced phonics programs in prior-to-school settings. *Contemporary Issues in Early childhood*, 15(1), 40–53.

Chiang, P.S. (2010). Home literacy education of Taiwanese Australian families: A sociological analysis. EdD thesis, QUT. http://eprints.qut.edu.au/43678/

Cope, B. & Kalantzis, M. (2009). 'Multiliteracies': New literacies, new learning. *Pedagogies: An International Journal*, 4(3), 164–95.

Dezuanni, M.L. & Woods, A.F. (2014). Developing media production skills for literacy in a primary school classroom: Digital materials, embodied knowledge and material contexts. In Georgina Barton (ed.), *Literacy in the Arts: Retheorising learning and teaching* (pp. 143–60). Switzerland: Springer International Publishing.

Exley, B., Woods, A. & Dooley, K. (2014). Thinking critically in the land of princesses and giants: The affordances and challenges of critical approaches in the early years. In J. Zacher Pandya and J. Ávila (eds), *Moving Critical Literacies Forward: A new look at praxis across contexts* (pp. 59–70). Oxford: Taylor & Francis.

Heath, S.B. (1982). What no bedtime story means: Narrative skills at home and school. *Language in Society*, 11(12), 49–76.

Hoffman, J.L. & Paciga, K.A. (2013). Click, swipe, and read: Sharing e-Books with toddlers and preschoolers. *Early Childhood Education Journal*. DOI: 10.1007/s10643-013-0622-5

Holdaway, D. (1979). *The Foundations of Literacy*. Sydney: Ashton Scholastic.

Hutchison, A., Beschorner, B. & Schmidt-Crawford, D. (2012). Exploring the use of the iPad for literacy learning. *The Reading Teacher*, 66(1), 16–23.

Jacobs, G.E. (2014). Reimagining multiliteracies: A response to Leander and Boldt. *Journal of Adolescent and Adult Literacy*, 57(4), 270–73.

Kalantzis, M. & Cope, B. (2012). *Literacies*. Cambridge: Cambridge University Press.

Leander, K. & Boldt, G. (2013). Rereading 'A Pedagogy of Multiliteracies'; Bodies, texts and emergence. *Journal of Literacy Research*, 45(1), 22–46.

Lloyd, S. (1992). *The Phonics Handbook*. Essex: Jolly Learning.

Luke, A. (2008). Pedagogy as gift. In J. Albright & A. Luke (eds), *Pierre Bourdieu and Literacy Education*. New York: Routledge.

Lynch, J. & Redpath, T. (2014). 'Smart' technologies in early years literacy education: A meta-narrative of paradigmatic tensions in iPad use in an Australian preparatory classroom. *Journal of Early Childhood Literacy*, DOI: 10.1177/1468798412453150

Marsh, J. (2005). The techno-literacy practices of young children. *Journal of Early Childhood Research*, 2(1), 51–66.

Marsh, J. & Yamada-Rice, D. (2013). Early literacy development in the digital age. In D.M. Barone & M.H. Mallette (eds), *Best Practices in Early Literacy Instruction* (pp. 79–95). New York: The Guilford Press.

Morgan, H. (2013). Multimodal children's e-books help young learners in reading. *Early Childhood Education Journal*, 41, 477–83.

Neumann, M.M. & Neumann, D.L. (2013). Touch-screen tablets and emergent literacy. *Early Childhood Education Journal*, DOI 10.1007/s10643-013-0608-3

New London Group (1996). A pedagogy of multiliteracies: Designing social futures. *Harvard Educational Review*, 66(1), 60–92.

Northrop, L. & Killeen, E. (2013). A framework for using iPads to build early literacy skills. *The Reading Teacher*, 66(7), 531–37.

O'Mara, J. & Laidlaw, L. (2011). Living in the iworld: Two literacy researchers reflect on the changing texts and literacy practices of childhood. *English Teaching: Practice and Critique*, 10(4), 149–59.

Paciga, K.A., Lisy, J.G. & Teale, W.H. (2013). Better start before kindergarten: Computer technology, interactive media and the education of preschoolers. *Asia Pacific Journal of Research in Early Childhood Education*, 7(2), 85–104.

Pahl, K. & Rowsell, J. (2005). *Literacy and Education: Understanding the new literacy studies in the classroom*. London: Paul Chapman Publishing.

Reutschlin Schugar, H., Smith, C.A. & Schugar, J.T. (2013). Teaching with interactive picture e-books in grades K-6. *The Reading Teacher*, 66(8), 615–24.

Roskos, K. & Neumann, S.B. (2014). Best practices in reading: A 21st century skill update. *The Reading Teacher*, 67(7), 507–11.

Rowsell, J. (2014). Toward a phenomenology of contemporary reading. *Australian Journal of Language and Literacy*, 37(2), 117–27.

Schugar, H.R., Smith, C.A. & Schugar, J.T. (2013). Teaching with interactive picture e-books in grades K-6. *The Reading Teacher*, 66(8), 615–24.

Serafini, J. & Youngs, S. (2013). Reading Workshop 2.0: Children's literature in the digital age. *The Reading Teacher*, 66(5), 401–4.

Simpson, A. & Walsh, M. (2014). Pedagogic conceptualisations for touch pad technologies. *Australian Journal of Language and Literacy*, 37(2), 128–38.

Street, B. (1984). *Literacy in Theory and Practice*. Cambridge: Cambridge University Press.

—— (1997). The implications of the 'New Literacy Studies' for literacy education. *English in Education*, 31(3), 45–59.

—— (2009). Ethnography of writing and reading. In D.R. Olson & N. Torrance (eds), *The Cambridge Handbook of Literacy* (pp. 329–45). Cambridge: Cambridge University Press.

Thoermer, A. & Williams, L. (2012). Using digital texts to promote fluent reading. *The Reading Teacher*, 65(7), 441–5.

Walsh, M. & Simpson, A. (2014). Exploring literacies through touch pad technologies: The dynamic materiality of modal interactions. *Australian Journal of Language and Literacy*, 37(2), 96–106.

Woods, A., Dooley, K., Luke, A. & Exley, B. (2014). School leadership, literacy and social justice: The place of local school curriculum planning and reform. In I. Bogotch and C. Shields (eds), *The International Handbook on Social [In]Justice and Educational Leadership* (pp. 509–20). New York: Springer.

Zipke, M. (2013). Building an e-book library. *The Reading Teacher*, 67(5), 375–83.

Chapter 2

Arts education and iPads in the early years

Sandra Gattenhof and Michael Dezuanni

Introduction

The term 'screenager' was coined 15 years ago by the author Douglas Rushkoff in his book *Playing the Future* (1999). He used the term to refer to young people reared from infancy on a diet of TV, computers and other digital devices. 'Screenager', like the term 'digital natives' (Prensky, 2001), aims to describe a generation that has never known a world without the internet or access to digital devices. More recently, Gardner and Davis (2013) have referred to the 'app generation' in an attempt to capture a sense of the differences between previous and present generations of young people's cultural experiences. In response to our almost ubiquitous technology-infused environment, it is not surprising that educators might wonder whether today's children and young people think and process information fundamentally differently from their predecessors. The generation gap certainly seems wider today as the amount of imagery and other media children encounter surpasses that of their parents and educators (Greenfield, 2004).

The cultural shift in children's lives – from reading books, playing with toys and watching television indoors and spending significant amounts of time outdoors, to experiencing much of life through digital media – has implications for children's cultures and all aspects of education (Marsh & Bishop, 2014). Edwards (2013) calls children's new forms of play 'post-industrial converged play', and she shows the relationships or 'webs' that are created between children's older forms of play, and newer digitally converged forms of play. The shifts in children's play are not necessarily negative and mobile technologies such as iPads are at the forefront of becoming the most innovative and dynamic tools in arts education. It is, therefore, timely to re-imagine the ways in which children can engage in arts experiences (both as artists and as arts theorists). The iPad can enable young children to create and share digital content that focuses on art forms and cross-curricular learning: for example children can explore drawing and painting, digital photography, digital storytelling, animation and more through the many arts apps available.

This chapter takes as a working premise that digital culture is embedded in the everyday life experiences of most children living in post-industrial societies, both in home and, increasingly, in educational contexts. We outline how our research project investigated strategies for developing learning in the arts for young children by using the iPad as a creative device, rather than one on which they consume content in the form of games, on-demand television and streaming video. We ask critical questions around creative ecologies and creative production; these grow from our observations on how young children and their families engaged with iPads through activities such as combining painting with digital photography. Analysis of work samples produced by children during the project enables interrogation of the ways in which young children can participate in arts practices and learning when digital media production is available. The chapter is structured around three themes of practice for iPad-based arts and creative education in preschool settings.

'Touch-screen' kids

There is a well-known video on YouTube called 'A Magazine is an iPad That Does Not Work' (2011). It shows a toddler engaging with an iPad, happily looking at and swiping through images. The same toddler is given a fashion magazine and tries to engage with the paper-based images in the same way. The magazine is similar in size to an iPad and the images just as glossy. But to the child's amazement the magazine is not interactive. In fact she checks that her finger is working by pressing it into her flesh and then trying it again on the magazine image. The behaviour of this child is not unique or surprising. According to Steyer (2013) 'we are seeing a fundamental change in the way kids consume media. Kids that can't even talk will walk up to a TV screen and try to swipe it like an iPad or an iPhone' (para. 5). The YouTube child and many others like her are products of what Hanna Rosin (2013) calls the 'touch-screen generation'; children are acquiring media literacies extremely early, alongside their usual verbal literacies and fine and gross motor skill developments. These examples show the extraordinary adaption by young children to smart technology, brought on by the high-speed growth and infiltration of interactive media into people's lives.

Rosin's (2013) coining of 'the touch-screen generation' along with Gardner and Davis' (2013) 'app generation' builds a picture of the cultural role of screen technologies heralded by Rushkoff's (1999) 'screenagers' and Prensky's (2001) 'digital natives'. Rosin, like Rushkoff and Prensky before her, is sniffing the wind of change. As she notes, 'American children have undergone a somewhat alarming transformation in a very short time' (Rosin, 2013, para. 4). While acknowledging that the change may be problematic for some researchers, educators and caregivers, Rosin notes that it is time to investigate 'that some good might come from those little swiping fingers' (2013, para. 5). A number of scholars have identified the ways in which children and young people's participation with digital technologies provides opportunities for them to participate and learn in digital culture through creative activity (Erstad, 2010; Erstad & Sefton-Green, 2013; Marsh, 2013).

According to American statistics (Neilsen, 2012) 70 percent of tablet-owning households with children under the age of 12 reported that their children use the device. In terms of dominance of usage it falls into two categories: to play downloaded games (77 percent) and for educational purposes (57 percent). These usage figures are echoed in a Common Sense Media Report (Rideout, 2013) that showed by age 8, 72 percent of children have used a smartphone, tablet or similar device. From this perspective, 'most children simply accept the ubiquitous place of technology as an unremarkable feature of life' (Green & Hannon, 2006, p. 44). One of the key findings from *Zero to Eight: Children's Media Use in America* (Rideout, 2013) was that children's access to mobile media devices is dramatically higher than it was two years ago. The report shows that:

> Among families with children age 8 and under, there has been a five-fold increase in ownership of tablet devices such as iPads, from 8% of all families in 2011 to 40% in 2013. The percent of children with access to some type of 'smart' mobile device at home (e.g. smartphone, tablet) has jumped from half (52%) to three-quarters (75%) of all children in just two years.
>
> (p. 9)

Children's increasingly early engagement with mobile devices has been confirmed in a number of research studies which show that children now enter preschool with predispositions for learning with digital technologies (Downes *et al.*, 2001; Goodwin, 2012). For children, says Angela Thomas (2006) 'there is no dichotomy of online and offline, or virtual and real; the digital is so much intertwined into their lives and psyche that the one is entirely enmeshed with the other' (p. 126). Many preschools do not yet have iPads freely available for children to use, so how might that availability affect their daily preschool activities, and particularly, how might iPads affect how children engage in the arts?

Australian early years learning framework and the national curriculum

One response to the children and young people's digital cultures has come from educational policy development. There are two key curriculum documents in the Australian education landscape that provide overarching frameworks for the inclusion of information and communication technologies in formal learning contexts for young children – the *Early Years Learning Framework* (Australian Government Department of Education, Employment and Workplace Relations, 2009) and the *Australian National Curriculum – The Arts* (ACARA, 2013). While neither document makes direct reference to the use of mobile technologies, both documents contain explicit statements about the inclusion of technologies in curriculum delivery.

The *Early Years Learning Framework*, covering 'learning from birth to five years and through the transition to school' (2009, p. 5), is structured through a sequence of outcome statements. Outcome 5 seeks to develop in young children the capacity to be effective communicators. Of the six teaching and learning contexts that expand upon this outcome, four statements have direct relevance to the uptake of mobile technologies:

> Children interact verbally and non-verbally with others for a range of purposes; Children engage with a range of texts and gain meaning from these texts; Children express ideas and make meaning using a range of media; and Children use information and communication technologies to access information.
>
> (p. 40)

Traditionally the definition of 'text' prescribes it as a linguistic structure woven out of words and symbols and often associated with physical books or even eBooks. Texts in an arts-based context go beyond the linguistic and symbolic, to include the plastic and the corporeal as identified by theorists such as Roland Barthes (1977) and Suzanne K. Langer (1953) who identify that a text includes anything that can be 'read' and interpreted including paintings, photographs and advertisements, dances and other performances. In taking Barthes's premise, 'texts' in an early childhood and arts context could include movement, music & sound, performance, visual art objects (2D, 3D and 4D), as well as film and photography. Media similarly is multi-textual and multi-textural because it includes digital technology practices executed in binary coding, plus potentially many creative art mediums.

Australian National Curriculum – The Arts takes up from where the *Early Years Learning Framework* finishes and spans learning from Foundation[1] to Year 10. The art forms included in the *Australian National Curriculum – The Arts* (2013) are dance, drama, media arts, music and visual arts. In scanning the content descriptors across the five art forms, direct reference to children manipulating technologies for artistic process and outcomes predominantly sit in the bands that cover upper primary and lower (junior) secondary for students aged between 10 and 14 years of age. A notable exception is to be found in the media arts strand in which the explicit inclusion of technologies begins at the Foundation level. Similar to the *Early Years Learning Framework the Australian National Curriculum – The Arts* contains seven overarching statements known as General Capabilities that are applied to all learning areas of the Australian National Curriculum. So while there may not be explicit statements about the inclusion of technologies within the content descriptions in the bands that apply to children in the early years of schooling (Foundation to Year 2; Year 3–4)[2] there is an expectation that teachers will include information and communication technologies in their learning activities. The formal inclusion of technologies across the learning areas is outlined in the statement about the general capability of Information and Communication Technology (ICT):

> Students develop ICT capability as they learn to use ICT effectively and appropriately to access, create and communicate information and ideas, solve problems, and work collaboratively in all learning areas at school, and in their lives beyond school. The capability involves students learning to make the most of the digital technologies available to them, adapting to new ways of doing things as technologies evolve and limiting the risks to themselves and others in a digital environment.
>
> In the Arts, ICT capability enables students to engage with digital and virtual technologies when making and responding to artworks. Students can, for example, use interactive multimedia platforms, communication and editing software, and virtual tools and environments, to design, create and share their artworks. They can enhance their ICT capability as they generate ideas and explore concepts and possibilities by exploiting available technologies.
>
> (ACARA, 2013, p. 20)

There are a number of important phrases in the statement that provide an arts educator with opportunities for classroom implementation of digital media technologies. The words 'create' and 'solve problems' appear, which means that the inclusion of digital technologies in the preschools, and indeed in all years of learning covered by the curriculum, should be used actively in the process of producing an artwork not merely as a process of documentation and dissemination. Likewise, the twinned key art production processes of 'making and responding' denote active engagement in both the construction process and 'reading' the work of others.

Arts education, twenty-first century style

The arts by their nature are interactional and '[s]tudents communicate ideas in current, traditional and emerging forms and use arts knowledge and understanding to make sense of their world' (ACARA, 2013, p. 3). Engagement in the arts is essentially a sensuous dialogue, a conversation between thoughts and feelings – head and heart – simultaneously (see O'Neill, 1995). Thomas (2006) argues that children's use of digital technologies provides 'interactionally dynamic discourses, cultures and spaces' for them (p. 129). Digital media is not governed by cultural identifiers so the tools (such as iPads) for making digital art provide children with platforms for open exploration of images, sounds and animations that allow them to explore their ideas and imaginings in expansive ways.

We now outline three themes that emerged from the project as we considered children's use of the iPad for arts learning.

Theme 1. Children's use of the technologies should complement not supplant physical arts engagement

Considering the almost ubiquitous position that mobile technologies now have on the lives of young children it seems necessary for arts educators, including preschool teachers, to include them in their curriculum programming. The influence that culture and society has on education sometimes becomes so widespread that it eventually forces a paradigm shift. A number of parents from our research project commented during interviews that they were supportive of the inclusion of iPads in the preschool curriculum. An Outer North Centre parent noted in a project interview the reason for this was because their children were 'getting the learning that they need to because I know a lot of schools these days are using them'. Parents now expect to see digital technology available and embedded into the preschool curriculum. Paradigm shifts are not trouble-free however: interviews with the early childhood educators involved in the project exposed some wrestling between support of digital technologies and concerns about the potential loss of the more familiar physical and concrete modes of learning such as using discovery and play-based approaches. Parents and educators alike saw the introduction of digital technologies as indicative of a high-quality learning programme as well as simultaneously desiring that overall, physical and concrete learning should remain the dominant pedagogy in early childhood. This contingent support for digital technologies also emerged in a research project that trialled the inclusion of iPads in learning activities for children in New South Wales schools (Goodwin, 2012). The research showed that teachers also supported the view that 'technology can complement traditional hands-on activities' (Goodwin, 2012, p. 69) but 'should not supplant them' (ibid.). The data from the trial indicated that the position of complementarity is particularly important in relation to 'students manipulating objects particularly in the creative arts curriculum area' (Goodwin, 2012, p. 69). The view that the use of iPads or any digital technology should not replace traditional hands-on arts engagement is supported by a sequence of research interviews undertaken by Holly Korbey (2013) of American arts teachers and artists for her blog post in *Mind/Shift* titled 'Paint or Paint App? Value of Creating Digital Vs. Traditional Art'. All teachers interviewed by Korbey agreed that:

> art made with the body using sensory, physical materials, is beyond valuable to understanding the artistic process, and should never be replaced (one Broadway dancer who teaches children's dance emphasized, 'Hands-on first, technology later.'). But all the same teachers also saw value in using the digital to enhance and even alter the act of creation.
>
> (Korbey, 2013, para. 16)

More broadly, individuals in the arts industry also recognise the need to engage with digital technologies. Matt Adams, one of the members of the

UK-based interactive performance group Blast Theory, who was 'thinker in residence' during the Adelaide Arts Festival in 2004 said:

> This is not to say that traditional theatre is finished. But in the same way that painting was transformed forever by the arrival of photography, it does have to change. Especially, if it seeks to reach a new, younger audience and to have cultural impact.

While Adams's address particularly references professional theatre practice targeted to the adult audience demographic, his sentiments can be equally applied to the inclusion of technologies, and in this case mobile technologies such as smartphones and tablets, in arts education for, by and with young children in the twenty-first century. Educators and arts professionals see the value of digital technology to enhance arts and creative activity, but they are mindful of the importance of maintaining physical, corporeal activity at the core of this. The influence of the inclusion of iPads in the construction process of visual art work, to 'alter the act of creation' (Korbey, 2013, para. 16), to enrich what might be possible over art produced with 3Dimensional materials can be seen in an interview with one of the preschool teachers involved in our project (2013):

Vignette I

T = preschool teacher
I = Interviewer (QUT Researcher)

T: So I guess just taking things as they arose and linking them into some drawing. We did some work around rhyme, so children were drawing rhymes. We took photos and the children added drawing to the photos. Perhaps that might be a photo of the garden or a photo of the playground and then the children adding their drawing over the top of that, overlaying the photo with drawing. But quite late in the term [a teaching assistant] started to overlay their art with drawing. So some children did a little bit of that.

I: So what did they do? They photographed their art work.

T: They painted whatever it was they painted and while it was on the easel we took a photo then brought it over [into the app] and they used the art program to draw on it. I think I recorded on some of those [as the children] told me what was happening and did some voice recordings on some of that as well.

The app used in this activity is called Draw & Tell (Duck Duck Moose, 2013). What is evidenced from this interview extract is that the preschool teacher was employing both concrete art-making processes involving paint and paper as well as mobile digital technologies simultaneously. This activity supports Goodwin's (2012) view that technology should not replace the traditional hands-on activities but be used alongside them. It is interesting to note in this extract that the teacher recorded the children's stories about the images they had constructed. This type of activity is not unusual in an early childhood setting but it usually occurs post-activity and handwritten by an adult rather than at the immediate time of making by the child. The Draw & Tell app enabled the child to create a unified artwork that integrated both spoken text and image. It allowed the child to understand that communication can be both verbal and non-verbal and encouraged the child to 'express ideas and make meaning using a range of media' (Australian Government Department of Education, Employment and Workplace Relations, 2009, p. 40). Using a plastic visual art medium (painting) and a digital communication medium (iPad) in this way demonstrates how the two media can work complementarily rather than the digital supplanting physical arts engagement.

Theme 2. Creating from scratch

Educational psychologist Jerome Bruner argues that the most beneficial learning state for a child is when learning is an active process and the child/student is directly involved in the manipulation of the content (Hannum, 2005, para. 6). Bruner classified the learning of a child as 'enactive, iconic and symbolic' (Bruner, 1966). Enactive learning is characterised by direct manipulation of objects without any internal representation of the objects, meaning children at a very young age classify objects in the world not by using words either spoken or written but by making gestures. From this perspective, tablet technology can be seen as an enabler for enactive learning as young children of preschool age can do things and interact with the world without speech or the written word.

There are a plethora of apps that allow for enactive learning, particularly associated with learning of the alphabet, letters sounds and numbers, and apps that can broadly fall into the categories of literacy and numeracy acquisition. However, Kate Highfield, lecturer at the Institute of Early Childhood at Macquarie University, believes apps, games or shows should help a child's development or keep them engaged in activities for longer. Highfield's (2013) research found 85 percent of the apps purchased by adults for children were drill and practice games that asked children to repeat an action or remember simple facts. Highfield states that such apps lead to lower-level neural development and often include excessive rewarding that can create unrealistic expectations in children. She recommends apps that require input from the child and in an arts-based context this means engaging with apps that allow young children to create something from scratch. An example of this might include apps that offer a blank surface that children then make an image on, or apps that require a child to select and create details to complete and activate an app. Preschool teachers in the QUT project also believed in the importance of children being able to make independent choices and decisions (with little or no restrictions) in the process of making art works in a variety of media. The following interview extract shows how the teachers in one preschool made deliberate choices to support the 'making from scratch' philosophy.

Vignette 2

T = preschool teacher
I = Interviewer (QUT Researcher)

T: The children have navigated the apps well. I guess we were qualifying after some time . . . we didn't want them to use stickers and things like that. So we were being more specific about what we wanted them to do.

I: I see it as a kind of similar situation whereby it's the difference if you're going to use the easel example, it's the difference between having an easel and brushes and paint and an easel with pre-cut shapes and cut out pictures from postcards and glue and stamps. And it's that, that's the difference. So just because it's digital, just shifting them away from pre-made images is always better. And so and you wouldn't do that, you wouldn't give them pre-made images, you would generally give them paints and brushes.

T: Sometimes we will, the collage-type stuff they can bring over to the painting as well. And use that as well.

I: I think and that certainly does happen but I think I mean I'm looking round your walls now, most of the stuff that you're declaring to the children that you like is pretty much completely hand generated. So you know there are no stickers in the images I can see and so to me that gives the children a clear message of these are the kinds of images that you like you know and these are the things that you enjoy of their work. So and of course it doesn't mean that you can't use certain things but I think you're saying to them it's great when you can come up with those ideas completely of your own you know. And I think by setting that as a challenge . . . it's a really nice way to stretch their thinking on it.

Apps such as Draw & Tell, Play School Art Maker, Paint & Draw, Popplet and Comic Life all allow young children to initiate a creative idea and take it through to finished artwork.

Theme 3. Quality learning requires intervention and redirection by adults

Vygotsky's educational theory of the zone of proximal development (ZPD) was developed at a time in which ICTs were not yet thought about and mobile digital technologies were more than 100 years from realisation.[3] The ZPD is defined as 'the distance between the actual developmental level as determined by independent problem solving and the level of potential development as determined through problem solving under adult guidance, or in collaboration with more capable peers' (Vygotsky, 1978, p. 86). Teachers use cooperative learning exercises where less competent children develop with help from more skilful peers or an adult – within the ZPD. Vygotsky believed that when a student is at the ZPD for a particular task, providing the appropriate assistance better enables the student to achieve the task. 'From a Vygotskian perspective, the teacher's role is mediating the child's learning activity as they share knowledge through social interaction' (Dixon-Krauss, 1996, p. 18). Early childhood educators 'take on many roles in play with children and use a range of strategies to support learning. They provide a balance between child led, child initiated and educator supported' (Australian Government Department of Education, Employment and Workplace Relations 2009, p. 15) learning episodes. Learning is undertaken in a supportive, play-based environment where experimentation, collaborative learning, problem solving and critical thinking are at the heart of the teaching and learning practices.

Within this teaching framework mobile digital technologies should be positioned as tools for learning and therefore the pedagogical approaches that teachers use in learning episodes with young children that do not engage technologies should not be absent from those episodes that do engage with technologies. To put it simply, 'students learn with technology not from technology' (Goodwin, 2012, p. 64). Early childhood educators engage in intentional learning – learning that 'is deliberate, purposeful and thoughtful' (Australian Government Department of Education, Employment and Workplace Relations, 2009, p. 15). Therefore, the process of learning employed by early childhood educators needs to continue to 'actively promote children's learning through worthwhile and challenging experiences and interactions that foster high-level thinking skills' (Australian Government Department of Education, Employment and Workplace Relations, 2009, p. 15) while within the technology frame. Thus, the ZPD, so important in enactive learning espoused by Jerome Bruner, should still be engaged to extend children's thinking and learning.

The preschool teachers in our project echoed the importance of rich discussions to deepen a child's learning experience. The following interview extract shows how one preschool teacher employed a ZPD approach across both learning engagement with paint & paper and with the iPad:

Vignette 3

T = preschool teacher

T: Some children who have really a lovely ability to draw cross over from work with pens, pencils and paints to iPads. Some children . . . who . . . might want to have a turn at the iPad (because it's the iPad) might be unsure of drawing . . . but I think they will possibly be the same children that would

> need to be talked through it and encouraged. They [the children] still need to talk through some of those strategies [related to drawing and painting].

Concomitant to the child-initiated activity that is supported by adult intervention a media teacher working as research assistant on our project supported and extended an incidental learning episode that occurred before the formal preschool programme began for the day. The media teacher informally introduced the children to the app Comic Life so that they were able to represent their story about the chickens in the preschool:

Vignette 4

MT = media teacher

MT: I sort of suggested things we could take photos of but I did not actually say you should take a photo of this or I didn't really help them with the framing of the photos or anything like that. I just let them take whatever photos they wanted to. But in saying that, some of the photos are really well framed so I didn't actually have to [intervene]. Once we've taken the photos I showed them how to use Comic Life and showed them how to add some photos that they took on their own. So once I showed them they then chose which photos they wanted and finished off the photo input. And then I explained that we could add some words then and so the students told me what they wanted to put for their sentences about the photos or about the chickens and I then typed them in for them. But they typed in their own names, so whenever their name came up they could type that in. And then they actually typed in each other's names at one point . . . and then created their own posters from that.

In this episode there are two sites of ZPD. One in which the teacher is working as a side-couch and supporter of the learning and a second where peer learning is in action when the children are writing their names onto the posters they had made in the app.

Both interview extracts demonstrate the importance of teacher intervention and redirection in deepening the learning experience for young children and that this type of engagement is no different if the experience utilises a tablet device or not.

Conclusion

The iPad was introduced to Australia on May 28, 2010 (Apple, 2010). 'The swift adoption of the devices in educational institutions indicates that teachers are eager to explore their potential in supporting student learning' (Goodwin, 2012, p. 22). This chapter has identified that for young children in preschool settings where iPads are present the experience of the 'live' and digital is characterised by convergence. Mobile digital technologies such as iPads are another tool where '[Y]ou can create something digitally that would be impossible to create by hand. Conversely, you can create something by hand that you cannot replicate digitally' (Korbey, 2013, para. 9). The employment of mobile digital technologies in preschools for the purpose of making and responding to artworks should not be a matter of the concrete activity over the digital one. The two experiences can have a symbiotic relationship in which one embellishes the other. However participation with these devices should not be undertaken without consideration to the learning context, in this case a preschool setting, in which adult-supported, discovery and play-based pedagogical approaches are used.

Notes

1 Across Australia the first year of school is variously referred to as preparatory (Queensland, Victoria & Tasmania), Reception (South Australia), Pre-primary (Western Australia), Transition (Northern Territory) or Preschool (New South Wales & Australian Capital Territory). For the sake of uniformity the Australian National Curriculum across all learning areas has adopted Foundation to identify the first year of schooling.
2 These bands cover children aged between 5 and approximately 9 years.
3 The iPad debuted in 2010 after beginning development by Apple in 2008.

References

Adams, M. (2004). 'Adelaide Thinkers in Residence Public Lecture.' Tuesday 16 March: Adelaide Town Hall.

Apple. (2010, May). Apple Press Info. Accessed June 22, 2014, from www.apple.com/au/pr/library/2010/05/07iPad-Available-in-Nine-More-Countries-on-May-28.html

Australian Curriculum, Assessment and Reporting Authority (ACARA) (2013, January). *Australian Curriculum: The Arts Foundation to Year 10.* Accessed January 14, 2014, from www.acara.edu.au/verve/_resources/Australian_Curriculum_The_Arts_2_July_2013.pdf

Australian Government Department of Education, Employment and Workplace Relations (2009). *Belonging, Being & Becoming: The early years learning framework for Australia.* Canberra: Commonwealth of Australia.

Barthes, R. (1977). *Image, Music, Text.* Selected and translated by Stephen Heath. London: Fontana Press.

Bruner, J.S. (1966). *Toward a Theory of Instruction.* Cambridge, MA: Belknap Press.

Dixon-Krauss, L. (1996). *Vygotsky in the Classroom. Mediated literacy instruction and assessment.* White Plains, NY: Longman Publishers.

Downes, T., Arthur, L. & Beecher, B. (2001). Effective learning environments for young children using digital resources: An Australian perspective. *Information Technology in Childhood Education Annual,* 1, 139–53.

Duck Duck Moose (2013) Draw and Tell. Duck Duck Moose. Accessed November 28, 2014, from www.duckduckmoose.com/

Edwards, S. (2013). Post-industrial Play: Understanding the relationship between Traditional and Converged Forms of Play in the Early Years. In A. Burke & J. Marsh (eds), *Children's Virtual Play Worlds: Culture, learning and participation*. New York: Peter Lang Publishing.

Erstad, O. (2010). Content in Motion: Remixing and Learning with Digital Media. In K. Drotner & K.C. Schroder (eds) *Digital Content Creation: Perceptions, practices and perspectives*. New York: Peter Lang.

Erstad, O. & Sefton-Green, J. (eds) (2013). *Identity, Community, and Learning Lives in the Digital Age*. London: Cambridge University Press.

Gardner, H. & Davis, K. (2013). *The App Generation: How today's youth navigate identity, intimacy, and imagination in a digital world*. New Haven, CT: Yale University Press.

Goodwin, K. (2012). *Use of Tablet Technology in the Classroom*. Strathfield: State of New South Wales, Department of Education and Communities.

Green, H. & Hannon, C. (2006). *Their Space. Education for a Digital Foundation*. London: DEMOS Foundation.

Greenfield, S. (2004). *Tomorrow's People: How 21st century technology is changing the way we think and feel*. London: Penguin.

Hannum, W. (2005). Jerome Bruner's Theory. *Learning Theory Fundamentals*. Accessed May 19, 2014, from www.theoryfundamentals.com/bruner.htm

Highfield, K. (2013, October) Do Educational Apps Enhance Your Child's Learning? *ABC Health and Wellbeing*. Accessed May 5, 2014, from www.abc.net.au/health/talkinghealth/factbuster/stories/2013/10/24/3874488.htm

Korbey, H. (2013, May). Paint or Paint App? Value of Creating Digital Vs. Traditional Art. *Mind/Shift*. Accessed May 14, 2013, from http://blogs.kqed.org/mindshift/2013/05/paint-or-paint-app-value-of-creating-digital-vs-traditional-art/

Langer, S.K. (1953). *Feeling and Form*. New York: Macmillan.

Marsh, J. (2013). Breaking the ice: Play, friendships and online identities in young children's use of virtual playworlds. In A. Burke & J. Marsh (eds), *Children's Virtual Play Worlds: Culture, learning and participation*. New York: Peter Lang Publishing.

Marsh, J. & Bishop, J.C. (2014). *Changing Play: Play, media and commercial culture form the 1950s to the present day*. New York: McGraw-Hill.

Neilsen (2012). *American Families See Tablets as Playmate, Teacher and Babysitter*. Accessed May 5, 2014, from www.nielsen.com/us/en/newswire/2012/american-families-see-tablets-as-playmate-teacher-and-babysitter.html

O'Neill, C. (1995). *Drama Worlds: A framework for process drama*. Portsmouth, NH: Heinemann.

Prensky, M. (2001). Digital Natives, Digital Immigrants. *On the Horizon*. MCB University Press, 9(5).

Rideout, V. (2013). *Zero to Eight: Children's media use in America*. San Francisco, CA: Common Sense Media. Accessed May 5, 2014, from www.commonsensemedia.org/research/zero-to-eight-childrens-media-use-in-america-2013

Rosin, H. (2013). The Touch-Screen Generation. *The Atlantic*. Accessed May 5, 2014, from www.theatlantic.com/magazine/archive/2013/04/the-touch-screen-generation/309250/

Rushkoff, D. (1999). *Playing the Future: What we can learn from digital kids*. New York: Riverhead Books.

Steyer, J. (2013, October). The Touchscreen Generation: 40 percent of kids under 2 years old have used a smartphone or tablet, study shows. *GMA News Online*. Accessed May 5, 2014, from www.gmanetwork.com/news/story/332882/scitech/technology/the-touchscreen-generation-40-percent-of-kids-under-2-years-old-have-used-a-smartphone-or-tablet-study-shows

Thomas, A. (2006). 'MSN was the next big thing after Beanie Babies': Children's virtual experience as an interface to their identities and their everyday lives. *E-Learning*, 3(2), 126–42.

Vygotsky, L.S. (1978). *Mind in Society: The development of higher psychological processes*. Cambridge, MA: Harvard University Press.

YouTube (2011, October). A Magazine is an iPad That Does Not Work. Accessed February 10, 2013, from www.youtube.com/watch?v=aXV-yaFmQNk

Chapter 3

Drawing and writing on the screen

Linda Knight and Karen Dooley

This chapter focuses on the physicality of the iPad as an object, how that physicality affects the interactions children have with the device generally, and how it might impact on the ways children draw and write on the iPad. Thinking about the physicality of the iPad in relation to drawing and writing is important because the materials, size, weight and appearance make the iPad quite unlike most other equipment in the preschool space. Most strikingly, this physicality does not literally convey the virtual vast dimensions of the iPad brought about through the diverse functions and contents of the apps contained in it. While the iPad is small enough and functional enough to be easily handled and operated even by young children, it is capable of performing highly complex, highly technological tasks that take it beyond its diminutive dimensions. Virtual–actual contrasts (the physical iPad as a contrast to the virtual worlds of games, and virtual pencils and paints) present interesting differences to the other resources more commonly found in a preschool space. While objects such as toys, bricks and building materials often do prompt the child to imagine and invent beyond the physical boundaries of the toy, they do not have the same types of virtual–actual contrasts of a digital device such as the iPad.

How then, might children be drawn to the iPad because of its physical, technological and virtual difference, and how might they negotiate drawing and writing on the iPad? How might children physically adapt to using digital surfaces? Might children forgo using paper and pencils, or learn new ways to explore writing and drawing? While the research project did not set out to compare how digital and paper-based resources affect writing and drawing skills there was great interest to see how young children managed drawing and writing on the shiny glass surface of the iPad.

Our research into early literacy development and how iPads encourage and prompt children to write and draw in ways that might differ to paper-based drawing and writing adds to a significant body of research into young children's emergent drawing and writing skills that primarily addresses paper-based drawing and writing (Anning and Ring, 2004; Reggio Children, 2001). The focuses of existing studies examine fine motor skill acquisition through the use of tools such as pencils, paintbrushes and scissors (Brookes, 1996; Schwake,

2012); critical/aesthetic/psychoanalytical analyses of the contents of drawings, stories, written texts (Cox 2013; Kiseleva *et al.*, 2014; Oğuz 2010); how/whether culture plays an influence on young children's drawings and writing (Bavin & Shopen, 2011; Crawford *et al.*, 2012; Einarsdottir *et al.*, 2009); as well as identifying/classifying developmental norms and disfunctions in children's drawings and writing (Galli *et al.*, 2011; Skibbe *et al.*, 2011; Stavy, 2012). Research into drawing and writing is clearly diverse in its alignment with development, education, creativity theories and agendas; however it lacks a commentary on children's use of digital technologies and the particular ways children negotiate writing and drawing as they use these technologies.

In this chapter we examine how the physicality of the iPad might affect how young children interact with it, including how they manipulate it as an object, how they might position it as they work and how they interact with the screen. A particular focus on how the young draw and write on the iPad offers up discussion on the use of skills to operate apps and incorporates public ideas about how iPad technology might affect the 'natural' writing and drawing development skills of young children.

Introduction

Given that desktop and laptop computers have far more technological capability and smartphones have almost identical capability, what is it about the iPad that makes it an object of desire to young and old, over the desire to own other digital devices? There have been five models of iPad since its launch in 2010; each development has focused on slimming down the size and weight of the device while increasing battery power, display clarity and functionality. The iPads used in the trial were iPad 3 devices; these measure 241.2 mm (H) × 185.7 mm (W) × 9.4 mm (D), and weigh 652g. These dimensions are similar to those of a print book, something Apple has made reference to in their marketing of the devices. The feel of an iPad is quite different from that of a book however. It is sleek and futuristic, with a metal back casing and a highly polished glass front screen. Where a book is flexible and sturdy, the iPad requires careful handling to avoid dropping it.

Despite its fragility, Apple has successfully marketed the concept of the iPad and its subsequent iterations to the public; this plays out in sales, estimated at around 200 million iPads as of June 2014 (Costello, 2014). Cleverly, Apple foregrounds the physicality of the iPad as a point of difference from other products and leverages their marketing on the form of the iPad in sleek and persuasive ways, noting that the device has been 'prepared from strong, beautiful materials like aluminum and glass . . . features that won't be found on a general PC' (Sahoo, 2012, p. 39). Because the iPad is presented as strong but highly manageable, even for young hands, we were interested to see how manageability might provide particular opportunities for drawing and writing differently to the ways children might draw and write on paper, blackboard or on a computer.

Striking a balance between technical sophistication, brand of choice and having wide appeal to both young and old has been a strong and successful marking strategy for Apple, not only with iPads, but with many of their products. Key to their marketing is the aesthetic styling of their advertising and how that in itself stands apart as a brand from the marketing of other similar products (Sahoo, 2012). As an example, the launch advertisements for the first two iPad models feature standard Apple marketing signatures of a talking head in front of a white background, plus isolated shots of the device against the same white background and accompanied by catchy music. The talking heads are high-level Apple employees; they are often male, in their 40s and present as being stylish and tech-cool with an easy and personable manner and possessing expert knowledge of the product. The device (iPad) is then featured without any other detail. It is highly polished and alluring as it slowly rotates. A key strategy is to have the device displaying the 'home screen' (this term alone has become synonymous with Apple products); the familiar visual of the home screen helps to connect the audience to the product because it is known and therefore suggests that the device will be easy to use.

The launch advertisement for iPad 1 took time, then, to feature close-range details of the iPad as it is being used for a range of purposes. These too are carefully chosen to appeal to a wide market: web browsing an online newspaper, reading an email that contains a photo of children and watching a children's movie. The over-shoulder shot carefully shows how the user confidently navigates through different functions with simple finger actions. Good image framing serves two purposes: it provides a visual tutorial to the new user and promotes the usability of the device as a toy to 'amplify the habits, conceits and fantasies we already had: enjoy music, play games, compose works of art, write novels, edit home movies' (Vaidhyanathan, 2011). The overall emphasis of the launch advertisement was to present the iPad as a revolutionary device that filled an unseen/unknown gap between the purpose of the computer (business, gaming, designing) and the smartphone (communication, gaming, photos, music) and via a functional design that was unlike either of those.

The iPad 2 launch also employed many of these signature marketing strategies, however Apple now introduced scene scenarios of 'real life' uses for the iPad, including a young child of around 2 years and its mother using the device together. The child touches the screen and seems to activate one of the apps, and the scenario continues with the child and its parents having a birthday party while distant grandparents watch via FaceTime©, an app that enables video streaming between Apple devices. The emphasis with iPad 2 is to demonstrate how easy it is to use, for the young to the old, and that the iPad is 'friendly' technology. As later versions of the iPad have been released (iPad 3 and 4, iPad mini, iPad air), the launch marketing continues to foreground these key aspects: size, weight, usability, and technical superiority – all in a highly recognisable brand design.

Apple's strong emphasis on gaining wide appeal coupled with their impeccable brand styling invokes a strong consumer desire to own Apple devices and thus 'become' tech-savvy-cool through ownership. Parents too, can be drawn in to consumer desire and this became evident when interviewing the parents in the three preschools, as many of them had purchased iPads; directly for use by themselves and indirectly for their children to use. Featuring children/ families in iPad marketing appeals to old and young consumers, and children too can desire to be tech-clever-smart. Apple's latest launch advert uses a pencil, laying on various types of tables in various types of rooms (including a classroom) to hide the presence of the iPad air; the association of the pencil as a primary/introductory writing implement makes an implied signification that the iPad is a device designed for learning by bright young minds.

The highly polished and effective marketing of the iPad, and the championing of its physical uniqueness has helped to establish the iPad as an object of desire that fulfils many criteria: fun for gaming, effective for social connectivity, efficient for working on, and cutting-edge for education and learning. Multi-capacity in such a sleek package sets the iPad apart from the more bulky laptop and desktop and the smaller screen of the smartphone and makes it an object that can be adapted easily into the preschool space.

The iPad in the preschool context

There was great excitement as the iPads arrived in each preschool; each centre had ten iPads to use. The staff quickly realised that the slim and smooth iPads might slip through children's hands easily so protective equipment was purchased for them. Chapter 8 discusses how each of the three preschools implemented protective measures to help staff relax about introducing the iPads to the children. Initially the staff at the preschools closely monitored the use of the iPads, often sitting with small groups of children to help facilitate safe use of the iPads as well as help the children become familiar with general operations and featured apps. The iPads gradually became more available in various ways. For example, six iPads were placed on a small table for children to sit at; the iPads were placed in a dedicated storage cupboard and freely available to children; children were able to sit on cushions with the iPad on their knee; and staff allowed children to take the iPads outside to capture images of the gardens and play areas.

The iPads were used more widely in the preschools as the management of them relaxed. At this point staff grew more aware of a need to shift their pedagogical practices due to the physical aspects of the device:

> I found that hard being first time users how to get comfortable with it. You know I could, just sitting it on my lap with kids everywhere just. . . . like I can't see it, I can't see it you know it was. . . . that physicality like you were saying it was awkward.
>
> (Interview with North Side preschool teacher)

The physicality of the iPads forced pedagogical changes. Ways to deal with a very smooth, reflective, flat screen were devised so that the educators could work with groups of children while watching other children at play (Figure 3.1). The educators adjusted their usual practices to accommodate a new learning material while maintaining their existing learning programmes.

In Figure 3.1 children sit in a circle with the iPads on the floor in front of them. The circle formation enabled the educator to observe all children at once as well as survey the room and other children playing elsewhere. Circular arrangements enabled the children to see the educator and other children clearly as well as observe the iPad activities of the other children. Social interactions, dialogic teaching and collaborative learning occurred, and the offer of help or advice was available if needed. Although this arrangement demonstrates effective problem solving with respect to dealing pedagogically with the technology, physically, it is an awkward image: the children seem to sit with poor posture and struggle to place the iPad functionally in front of them. The variations in positioning suggest that each child is not able to fully reconcile the object; their legs look awkward and their positions might not be sustainable for long. Concerns about the postural damage caused by long-term use of the iPad, along with other digital devices, were voiced by parents and educators:

Figure 3.1 Children learning to use iPads

R1: I think posture could be bad
R2: Posture yeah
R1: I mean some of where I like leaned over a lot more than I'm happy with. And it's only when he's on the iPad for a long time.
R2: Yeah, yeah, yes that thing of head down and . . .

So although the parents and educators were interested in having the iPads come into the preschool, their enthusiasm was tempered by thoughts of protecting the children physically from potential harm. The influence of various pedagogical movements and approaches act as warning voices that fuel protection discourses. These can include those of the Steiner education movement (Childs, 1991), the unschooling approach (Griffith, 2010), and outdoor/natureschooling (Stone, 2009) that caution against childhoods tainted by too much technology (Payne, 2009), stifled by too much static activity (Miller *et al.*, 2004) or isolated by insular, solitary activity (Subrahmanyam *et al.*, 2001):

> R: That's my biggest problem with it I think and in Kindy, I love Kindy. I think that Kindy is really value adding to the 4-year-old and in that if he's sitting there with an iPad he's not doing something really valuable and creative and stimulating.
>
> (Interview with a parent)

The albeit muted presence and influence of these warning voices seemed to play out in the ways that the educators tried different arrangements and scenarios until both they and the children felt literally and pedagogically comfortable with using the devices. Similar negotiations of the physicality of the device occurred when the children took them home to work with their families and carers.

As an object, the iPad can serve different purposes to users: as implied in the Apple advertisements, the iPads made high-tech-cool play possible for children at home and preschool; the iPad, as an affordable piece of desirable, high-functioning technology that everyone from CEOs to schoolchildren are seen with was accessible to all the preschool children and their families; and conversely, there was concern that iPads might ruin a natural, 'organic' or slow-pace childhood. Observing the use of iPads in the preschool space by young children, their families and educators helped expose how some of the ways that the iPad is regarded and used played out on a micro scale.

Drawing and writing on the iPad

In focusing on the iPad as a physical object and how its materiality might affect the ways in which children write and draw, we engage with popular interest into the potential educational benefits for children using an iPad. Specifically, the project examined how writing and drawing might be done differently on the smooth glass surface of the iPad, as compared to the ways children write and draw with physical tools and materials such as paper, blackboards, whiteboards, pavements and other surfaces.

As already discussed, the physicality of the iPad meant it was used pedagogically, in generative ways by adults and children. As an example, one of the preschools commented on how they and the children actively sought out micro-solutions to each learning experience, depending upon the nature and the purpose of the activity:

> R: iPad learning activities . . . independently, with guided instruction, individually. There are still some who need that. And in pairs or small groups I've just started doing that with the photography. But we have done group work, whole group work as well. We haven't done like small groups of four or five at a time with something. It's either been independent or in pairs when they did the photography or whole group full of intentional teaching.
>
> (Interview with South Side preschool teacher)

The educator explains how her usual pedagogical practices take on a greater flexibility and experimentation. Her words also suggest that the usual power

Figure 3.2 Children and educator exploring iPads

relationships of educator and child are shifted because the unfamiliarity of the media allows everyone to explore together how the iPads might be used for different purposes. We are not being idealist in our interpretation of the teacher's words; the subjective power relationships between educator and children still remain, however the arrival of the iPads brings some slippage and disruption to these relationships as adults and children collectively discover and experiment.

A common way to write and draw on the iPads was to have children sit with an educator at a table for short periods of time. In Figure 3.2 the educator sits with a small group of children around a table under cover in the outside area of the preschool. Verandas are a common area for activity in Australia's relatively warm climate; many Australian preschools have large covered patio areas that are used as an in-between indoor/outdoor space and to provide shade from the sun and heat. As with the circle arrangement shown in Figure 3.1, the children in Figure 3.2 are organised in such a way to enable solitary working, communication with the educator and each other, and a clear view of each iPad. Physically the children seem more comfortable, their posture is improved and they are able to work with greater control.

In this particular drawing and writing episode the educator drew on task-focused, direct teaching pedagogies to explain to the children how to use the new drawing or writing app. As children explored the app and asked questions, she was able to suggest techniques and options for using the different functions of the app. Because children could come and go from the table, the educator repeated the same instructions each time a new child came to participate. The pedagogic settings here are similar to those described in Chapter 1: children have the freedom to select an activity but teachers use direct instruction to support the operation of the device and apps.

The effectiveness of particular pedagogical approaches encouraged educators to reuse them. For example when the educator used direct teaching to introduce the children to a new drawing app (Doodlecast) her explicit description of the sequential steps of how to open and navigate through the app and how to use each of the functions helped the children experiment with various tools and options to produce their digital work. Crucially, the educator consciously used the correct terminology for apps and general iPad functions, including 'home button', 'share', 'export', 'swipe' and others. Children then verbally repeated the terminology and applied it, which aided collective learning of the technology by adults and children.

These small group drawing and writing activities were similar in many ways to paper-based drawing and writing; the educator did not tell the children what to draw or write but responded to their ideas as they occurred. Direct instruction was limited to device and app operation; content remained under child control. Children did seek assistance if the app confused them but otherwise worked independently. When the children produced work and wanted to discuss it, the educator would likewise take the opportunity to extend those discussions.

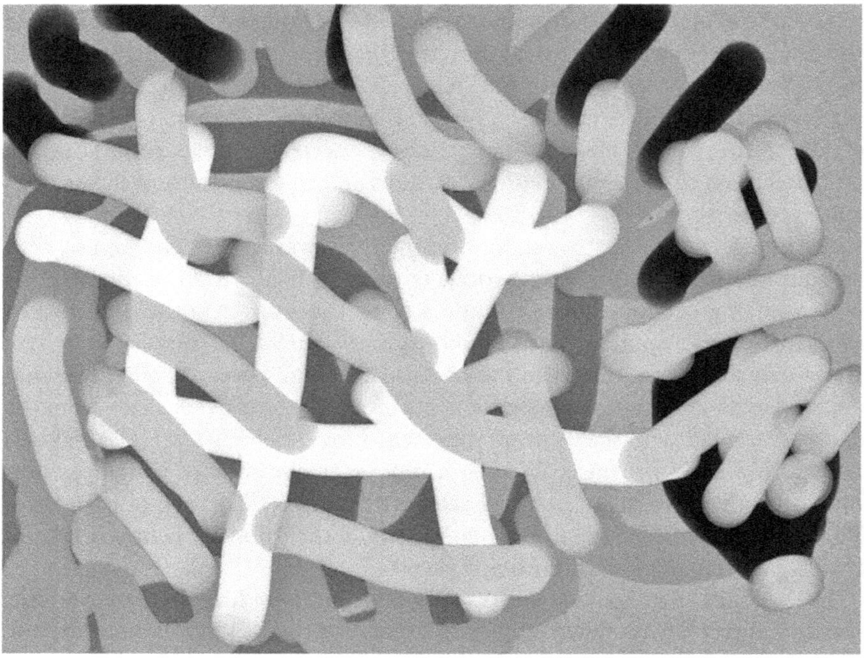

Figure 3.3 Digital drawing
Brushes app: free.libre open source software
Reprinted by permission of QUT Legal

During these discussions all the children usually stopped using the iPads so that they could contribute before recommencing with their work.

Two examples of the writing and drawing work produced (Figure 3.3 and Figure 3.4) demonstrate the particularities of digital-based work, compared to the possibilities afforded by paper-based drawing and writing (Figures 3.5 and 3.6). The saturated colour of the digital imagery highlights an obvious difference between the two types of work. Our focusing on colour difference could be regarded as a superficial analysis of children's art that likely contains many more meanings, however it is worthy of mention because the bright and saturated colour on a smooth glass iPad screen did encourage children to persist with performing the writing and drawing tasks. We do not aim to compare or promote children using iPads over paper, however the digital examples produced by the children during the study suggest that children were highly motivated to create text-based and image-based 'work' on the iPad (as a point of difference to the 'play' things they produced in game-based apps). The effects generated through the colour and tool options in apps were very attractive to the children. As an example, some children liked to saturate the screen by covering it with wide lines of colour until they made a new colour page; other children made complex line patterns via a combination of lines and marks, as seen in Figure 3.3.

Children became more experimental with their ideas as they realised they could easily erase the mistakes they made on the iPad; they were able to edit various aspects of their work by using functions such as the undo or erase button until they were happy with their efforts. In the Doodlecast app children took a lot of pleasure exploring subtle and garish colour/pattern contrasts by selecting highly patterned backgrounds and photographs as their starting point and then drawing onto those with equally bright colours. The opacity of the colours meant that children could clearly see the contrasts and could spend time thinking about the effects of these contrasts as well as the contents of their work. Their awareness of the effects of colours and their quick uptake of the editing functions supported their developing aesthetic awareness, to reveal 'a world he or she may not have noticed but that is there to be seen if only one knew how to look' (Eisner 2008, p. 11). While there is clear benefit in children being able to ponder these choices in a more corporeal sense by physically handling tools, or exploring the viscosity of paints, or the texturality of the paper when drawing and writing by hand, decisions about editing or altering marks can be more difficult to achieve with the more permanent materials (paint, oil pastel, pencil) used in paper-based work.

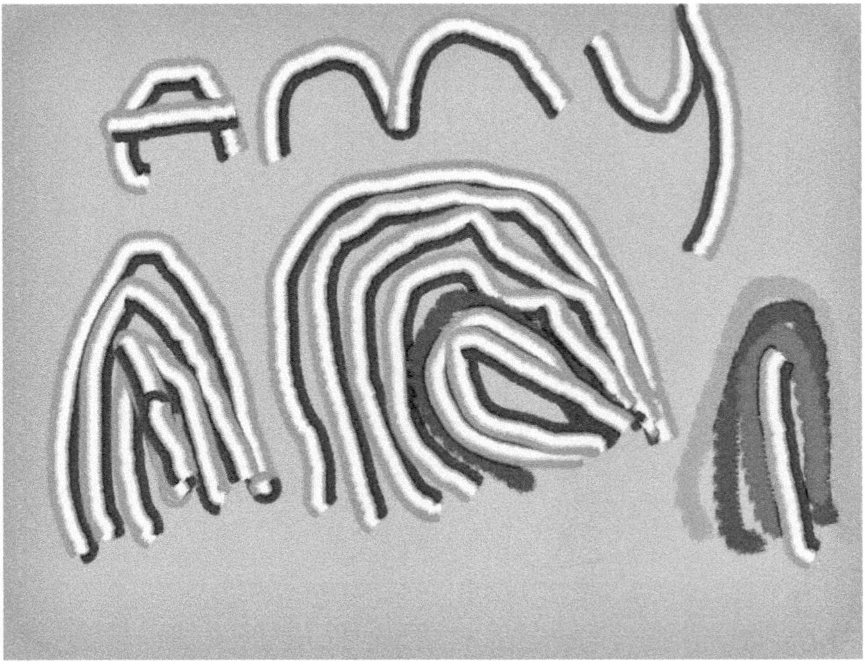

Figure 3.4 Digital writing

Figure 3.5 Paper-based writing and drawing

Figure 3.6 Paper-based handwriting exercise

The initial instruction the educators gave to children enabled more independent trialling and exploring of digital drawing and writing techniques (such as using the finger to make lines on a chosen background). Children were also shown how to save their work into the photos folder for later uploading onto the preschool computer. While independent working is a positive element of using iPads in preschools, the educators were sometimes concerned that they could not see what the children were working on, particularly when children produced images or completed tasks but then preferred to delete rather than save their work. Often if children deleted work they did so very quickly and before showing work to an adult.

The small act of deleting work raises issues about exposure and privacy and how children's efforts to draw and write have become heavily scrutinised. iPads can make the mistakes and trials of the children less accessible to teachers as they are learning to draw and to write. The scribbles, erasings, misspelt words and reversed letters produced very obviously on paper provide educators with important information about the child's developing skills and comprehension; these are rendered almost invisible on the iPad because the child can quickly erase mistakes and begin again without the educator having seen anything. An obvious answer is to always provide a mixture of paper-based as well as digital-based opportunities for children to write and draw; however the point raises a bigger issue: who actually benefits from the need to see what children produce? Certainly, a child benefits from working alongside an adult, even though children are also highly capable of learning independently through repetition of a task (additionally, repetitive tasks on an iPad are enjoyable, the visual effects are attractive and children quickly learn to perform them correctly). The benefit to the adult has more to do with gaining information about the child than the adult learning a new skill. A large portion of a contemporary early childhood educator's daily routine has to do with observation, recording and reporting (Ortlipp *et al.*, 2011). The systems of reporting and accrediting in place in contemporary preschools force educators to scrutinise behaviours and productions, hence their concern around children using a device which allows for the quick deletion of work without it being seen by an adult. Putting iPads in preschools can present an unanticipated challenge to the habits of surveillance over what children learn and how they learn it, and how available that is to the adults and education system around them.

Modes and politics of drawing and writing on the iPad

Beyond issues of observation and reporting, using iPads for drawing and writing also exposes conventional and normative thinking about how children should physically draw and write. Having young children digitally explore writing and drawing encouraged the educators and parents to consider the physical conventions around those skills and what an iPad does to subvert those. The general public and popular press have not embraced comfortably the prospect of very young children using iPads to write and draw, suggesting that 'tech-savvy kids can't push a pencil' (Starke, 2013). Fear of children not learning the correct 'pencil-grip' for writing (not drawing; good drawing skills require a different handling of a pencil) because they are spending too much time using their fingers to write on an iPad is symptomatic of a contemporary society conflicted between the lure of technological possibilities and the upholding of traditional skills. In particular, it reflects anxiety about the capacity of children to take high-stakes, pen-and-paper national literacy tests later in their school career.

The children in the preschools utilised their fine motor skills by using their index finger as a stylus. Because the iPad screen is touch-sensitive, children quickly learnt to effectively point their index finger on the screen while holding their thumb and other fingers away from it (evidence of hand postures can be seen in Figures 3.1 and 3.2). Children also used their dominant hand to work on the iPads; i.e. they used the same hand to write on the iPad as well as to write with a pencil. Children also improvised and used their hands and fingers in other ways:

> R: I have noticed some children won't always use their fingers. Some are using a thumb to touch buttons and that sort of thing. So while they're still probably using their dominant finger they are quite comfortable using another digit.
>
> (Interview with North Side preschool teacher)

The children demonstrated highly developed fine motor and gross motor skills as they manipulated their hands and fingers to perform the writing and drawing tasks in the apps. Their skill in using the iPads showed how technology can actively support fine and gross motor skill development while also contesting conventions about what type of activities best facilitate such learning (O'Mara & Laidlaw 2011). The drawing and writing apps preferred by the children (Reading Eggs, Doodlecast, Draw and Tell) were selected by choice and visited repeatedly. These apps were visually compelling; however, attraction was partnered by the children's desire to repeatedly perform the physical activities in each app. iPads therefore can be seen to possess a digital and physical materiality in that they direct minute, repetitive corporeal interactions that are equally restrictive (the app perpetuates repeated movements each time it is used) and unrestrictive (the digital platform actively contests the norms and conventions around how best to develop the fine motor skills needed for writing and drawing).

When asked about drawing and writing on the iPad, the children conveyed how comfortable they were with using their fingers to perform writing and drawing tasks:

I: So when you draw on the iPad is that different to drawing on a piece of paper?
R: Yes
I: How is it different?
R: Because . . .
R2: Because you just use the finger and draw like that . . .
R: Then you draw you umm you put your finger on the paper and it's different to using your hands.
I: Yeah is it easier or harder?
R: It's easier.

I: It's easier is it to draw on the iPad?
R: Yes it's way easier, this way's easier.

The enthusiasm demonstrated by the children, was taken up by the educators and they developed ideas for using the drawing and writing programs in wider contexts. Their willingness to experiment was highly positive considering how early childhood teachers and professionals can hold well-cemented ideas about drawing and writing skills instilled by the official language of policy and curriculum documents. Such conservatism also influences how those 'outside' the system frame their understandings about growth and development; parents and carers can adopt the same developmentalist terminologies as the 'experts':

> R: Well what he's loved particularly has been the Reading Eggs, star, letter recognition and the drawing of the letters and the dot to dots. And that's really suited him. He's left-handed and has poor fine motor.
>
> (Interview with a parent)

At times these professional/non-professional lines can blur so parents who are also educators can add extra layers of expectation about what their children should be doing at preschool. In one of the preschools the educators were aware of the pressures that having a teacher-parent placed them under, in terms of learning expectations:

> R: . . . why perhaps would we be encouraging children to use their fingers to trace letters when perhaps more desirably we should be getting them to use a stylus and honing those fine motor skills . . . tracing letters, that was her thoughts about that.

Despite these concerns, in the main, parents and carers were interested in their children exploring iPads for learning and were curious about how writing skills in particular might be enhanced through the device:

> R: He's really good; he's quite good with the pencils. So I'd rather get him on a pencil like but my older child who actually does have poor fine motor skills, that might have been helpful when he was four to do that. Something that I'd never do any other way maybe some finger painting or something that might have helped him to develop it more gradually because it didn't come as naturally for him.
>
> (Interview with a parent)

Collectively the parents, carers and educators were interested in learning about the ways iPads might enhance more formal drawing and writing processes and how iPads can motivate children to exercise their hand and motor skill dexterity. The enthusiasm the children showed for 'doing' writing and drawing, perhaps to a level not anticipated by parents and teachers, fuelled parent's interest in the project. When asked, children clearly articulated their preferences for particular apps:

I: What do you like doing most on the iPad?
R: Playing games and drawing letters

And:

I: Oh. Okay is there anything you want to learn to do on the iPad?
R: Ahh yes
I: What's that?
R: Draw letters
I: You want to be able to draw the letters, what about you [name]?
R1: I want to be able to draw the letters

The three preschools began to explore ways for drawing and writing with the iPad, in addition to the more familiar paper-based activities. Rather than isolate these activities, the educators found creative ways to weave and connect the iPad to other aspects of preschool learning and activity. Combining photography and drawing, or creating paintings on paper and then photographing them so they can be worked on further in iPad apps were some of the ways that children began to make connections between creating and merging 2Dimensional (such as work produced with a pencil and paper) and digital work. The educators began to understand how the iPad need not be used in place of handmade drawing, but alongside it and with it. In one particular instance the iPads were used to connect children to their learning environment with drawing. Drawings were created on different topics and then the children told stories about the drawings and used storybooks to add to their narratives. The storybooks then became an influence for further iPad drawings and children were encouraged to describe why they liked the story. Programming became more fluid and emergent as the educators investigated and trialled ways to weave iPad drawing and writing into their regular programs:

> R: Just taking things as they arose and linking them into some drawing. We did some work around rhyme, so children were drawing rhymes. We umm took photos and the children added drawing to the photos. Perhaps that might be a photo of the garden or a photo of the playground and then the children adding their drawing over the top of that, overlaying the photo with drawing. But quite late in the term [name] started to overlay their art with drawing. So some children did a little bit of that.
>
> (Interview with North Side preschool teacher)

Exposure and experimentation enhanced aesthetic and creative skills also, so that the educators were developing what Eisner (1998) calls their 'connoisseurship' around understandings of composition, balance and detail in visual imagery: it became less of a mystery to the educators as they spent time with the apps and devices. Knowledge translated to the discussions they had with the children about the drawings being made:

> R: If you're choosing a thick pencil, a thick paint brush perhaps . . . you might run out of room or you might only get half of your butterfly in or the butterfly but not the flower. But if you choose something with a finer line then you might get more detail in the space . . . talking about making those choices about the medium that you're using.
>
> (Interview with North Side preschool teacher)

Their willingness to explore the iPad technology-in-action exposed the educators to some unexpected possibilities for its use:

> R: Some children I think maybe don't go to easels a great deal but might come to the iPads to draw.

Suddenly the iPad could be a site for drawing and writing for children who, for different reasons, have oversensitivity to tactile materials such as clay, paint, chalk, water, mud etc. Educators noticed how children with tactile sensitivity liked the smooth glass surface of the iPad and the virtual opportunities it provided to make art, draw and write. It opened up spaces for learning that had not been taken up by those children before. Through finding ways to integrate iPad drawing and writing into the preschool for these children, the educators became more inclusive in their thinking of the iPad as a tool for learning, for children with differing skills and needs.

Discussion

Observations of children's physical interactions with drawing and writing apps on iPads made during the study enable critical discussion of how digital technology might be used positively with young children.

Clearly, there are contrasts between paper-based and digital-based writing and drawing, not least because the tools and surfaces that are used are completely different. What has emerged through the drawing and writing work produced by children, and the thoughts and reflections provided by parents, educators and children is that both modes benefit and develop a child's drawing and writing skills. They use paper and iPads in complementary ways which collectively assists in nurturing the gross and fine motor skills needed for writing and drawing development.

iPads and paper-based work each help to develop connoisseurship, or an aesthetic education. While our study did not aim to establish whether iPads enhanced aesthetic awareness more so than paper-based work, the study exposed how educators, parents and particularly children demonstrated enhanced acuity in relation to colour, contrast, pattern, purpose, composition, line and balance in drawn imagery, and line, form and balance in written imagery. Participants did not actively mention a growing aesthetic awareness; however, their reflections on the project often alluded to increased awareness of image quality and enhancing their drawing and writing capacities:

> R: I like most things to be creative . . . you know they need to be able to write their letters and they need to be able to recognise them. It's providing another creative way of exposing them to learning them, particularly the touch and feel direction of those two programs that we've got on there, that's important.
>
> (Interview with South Side preschool teacher)

While iPads cannot claim to enhance aesthetics over paper-based media, the availability of editing and reversing aspects of a drawing or writing on the iPad may provide more time for children to focus on the composition of their work above spending time correcting lines and marks, or removing colour strokes.

Importantly, the technological abilities of the iPad to edit and erase provided children with intellectual space to develop critical and analytical skills. Children were very happy to erase work they were not satisfied with rather than to persist with drawing or writing that was not working well. The child's freedom to erase their work was quite troubling to some of the educators; this raises discussion about the romanticised valorisations adults can hold about children's early paper-based drawings and writing, and why these early attempts with their disorganisation and muddy colours are held in higher regard than the smoother images produced on a digital tablet. The paper-based images that young children produce have large amounts of sentiment attached to them, which is not really connected to the value of the work but more the appearance. Those appraisals suggest that paper-based work is actually more beneficial (in terms of its educational value) to a child than a digital image. Perhaps one reason for the uncertainty about whether the work produced on an iPad is as educationally valid as paper-based work has to do with conventional notions of authenticity and the 'real' learning processes young children should navigate:

> R: I've got a child in my class who does the spelling test on an iPad because his fine motor is atrocious and it will take him three years to write the ten spelling words. He just drags the letters down. Okay if I had a child who was . . . 'all I have to do is not form my letters correctly and I can use the iPad', that concerns me.
>
> (Interview with a parent)

iPads introduce children to digital drawing and writing in stimulating ways; however, currently there remains some scepticism by adults about whether children are engaging in 'real' learning in comparison to the more conventional and familiar efforts produced on sheets of paper. In our study children created drawings and writing that were highly praised by the educators, parents and carers involved in the study so it would seem that adults can adjust their regard for iPads through close exposure to how children actually use them. Certainly the enthusiasm demonstrated by the children suggests that the repetitive actions in apps motivated them to persist with learning how to form letters and simple words, and in controlling the drawing of a line to write letters and draw pictures:

> I: So did he have a preference; of all of the apps that you had did he show a preference?
> R: Mainly the letters one, the tracing one.
>
> (Interview with a parent)

As adults get more exposure to iPads, and as they gather understandings of how young children can use them, populist perceptions about iPads do begin to shift. Mistrust gives way to cautious curiosity:

> R: And or if I want to teach him to write he can go, he's really good, he's quite good with the pencils. So I'd rather get him on a pencil like but my older child who actually does have poor fine motor skills, that might have been helpful when he was four to do that.
>
> (Interview with parent)

Greater awareness of the diverse ways that children can learn to write and draw might lessen the fear around their exposure to digital media. Fears about digital media signalling the end of educational quality and the loss of early childhood innocence begin to dissipate when parents, carers and educators experience how children can use digital media without forgetting about or forsaking other toys, games and activities. Watching how children use iPads can be challenging because the introduction of a new media does bring about changes to the usual sequences of learning children progress through in their acquiring of writing and drawing skills:

> R: I said to [name] can you sign your name? And he said yeah and he picked up a pen and it was the first time that I'd really paid a lot of attention to him holding a pencil. And . . . he had no control over what it was doing and he goes I don't need to write my name I can do it on the iPad. I said no, no you need to write with the pen as well. But . . . he could do exactly what he wanted with his fingers on the iPad but holding a pencil his pencil grip was atrocious [Laughs].
>
> (Interview with parent)

Rather than sounding alarm bells, this quote by a parent demonstrates that children are highly able to adapt their skills for different tasks. Children will still continue to learn to use hand-held tools such as pencils and paintbrushes, now however they also learn to use their finger as a stylus for digital learning. Parents, carers and educators begin to understand that the content of education is not fixed: one new thing will not replace the old. iPads are now increasingly regarded as having a useful place in education but will never replace some experiences:

> R: the skills of handwriting, the skills of touch, the skills of contact, like you said about that, she's got somebody reading to her. Yeah but she hasn't. She's got a machine reading to her.
>
> (Interview with a parent)

The children in our study physically adapted to using digital surfaces, and their conceptual understandings of writing and drawing grew through use of the iPads (Gruber *et al.*, 2012). They did not forget or resist using paper and hand-held materials, they simply expanded on the ways they like to explore writing and drawing.

Conclusion

The reflections and observations on children's forays into writing and drawing on iPads prompt some summarising commentary about the norms and conventions around children's development and growth and becoming 'school-ready' (Lynch & Redpath, 2012) in early childhood education and care. Our observations during our project cause us to think about how the expectations that educators, parents and carers might hold around drawing and writing milestones can be informed and shaped by institutionalised practices and understandings of children's development. The chapter also shows how chinks often appear in convention; the data expose how children, educators and their families experimented with digital writing and drawing in ways that seem to confound expectations and assumptions.

While the children and adults enjoyed using the iPads in our study, they were not totally besotted; neither the children nor adults proclaimed they would only work on iPads from now on: they remained invested in continuing to use paper and hand-held tools to draw and write. It was interesting to see how the children particularly could take or leave the iPads, even when they were freely available. Many children did not play with the iPads at all but preferred to play with other things available in the centres.

The fears held by the general public around iPads ruining children's learning by initiating isolated, static activity were not evidenced in our project. The images that pepper the popular press featuring young children sitting in front of computers and not communicating with each other were not enacted in the preschools. Instead the children collaborated and shared in the same ways that they use other materials together. Their efforts at writing and drawing were also collaborative, active and creative with children advising and working as a group to learn the apps and create their images. In this respect iPads serve a highly functional and educational role in a child's writing and drawing development.

References

Anning, A. & Ring, K. (2004). *Making Sense of Children's Drawings*. Berkshire: McGraw-Hill International.

Bavin, E.L. & Shopen, T. (2011, October). The development of narrative by Warlpiri children. *Proceedings of the Annual Meeting of the Berkeley Linguistics Society*, 11.

Brookes, M. (1996). *Drawing with Children: A creative method for adult beginners, too*. Los Angeles, CA: J.P. Tarcher.

Childs, G. (1991). *Steiner Education in Theory and Practice*. Edinburgh: Floris Books.

Costello, S. (2014). What are iPad sales all time? http://ipod.about.com/od/ipad modelsandterms/f/ipad-sales-to-date.htm Accessed 19 June 2014.

Cox, M.V. (2013). *Children's Drawings of the Human Figure*. Hove: Psychology Press.

Crawford, E., Gross, J., Patterson, T. & Hayne, H. (2012). Does children's colour use reflect the emotional content of their drawings? *Infant and Child Development*, 21(2), 198–215.

Dennis, L.R. & Votteler, N.K. (2013). Preschool teachers and children's emergent writing: Supporting diverse learners. *Early Childhood Education Journal*, 41(6), 439–46.

Einarsdottir, J., Dockett, S. & Perry, B. (2009). Making meaning: Children's perspectives expressed through drawings. *Early Child Development and Care*, 179(2), 217–32.

Eisner, E.W. (1998). *The Enlightened Eye: Qualitative inquiry and the enhancement of educational practice*. Upper Saddle River, NJ: Prentice Hall.

—— (2008). Art and knowledge. In J.G. Knowles and A.L. Cole (eds), *Handbook of the Arts in Qualitative Research*. Los Angeles, CA: Sage. 3–12.

Galli, M., Vimercati, S.L., Stella, G., Caiazzo, G., Norveti, F., Onnis, F. & Albertini, G. (2011). A new approach for the quantitative evaluation of drawings in children with learning disabilities. *Research in developmental disabilities*, 32(3), 1004–10.

Griffith, M. (2010). *The Unschooling Handbook: How to use the whole world as your child's classroom*. London: Random House LLC.

Gruber, T., Meixner, B., Prosser, C. & Sick, B. (2012). Handedness tests for preschool children: A novel approach based on graphics tablets and support vector machines. *Applied Soft Computing*, 12, 1390–98.

Kiseleva, N.A., Kalinina, R.R. & Kovalevskaya, E.V. (2014). Emotional and cognitive characteristics of children living in the SOS children's village. *Middle-East Journal of Scientific Research*, 20(12), 2105–8.

Lynch, J. & Redpath, T. (2012). 'Smart' technologies in early years literacy education: A meta-narrative of paradigmatic tensions in iPad use in an Australian preparatory classroom. *Journal of Early Childhood Literacy*, 14(2), 1–28.

Miller, J., Rosenbloom, A. & Silverstein, J. (2004). Childhood obesity. *The Journal of Clinical Endocrinology & Metabolism*, 89(9), 4211–18.

Oğuz, V. (2010). The factors influencing children's drawings. *Procedia-Social and Behavioral Sciences*, 2(2), 3003–7.

O'Mara, J. & Laidlaw, L. (2011). Living in the iWorld: Two literacy researchers reflect on the changing texts and literacy practices of childhood. *English Teaching: Practice and Critique*, 10(4), 149–59.

Ortlipp, M., Arthur, L. & Woodrow, C. (2011). Discourses of the early years learning framework: Constructing the early childhood professional. *Contemporary Issues in Early Childhood*, 12(1), 56–70.

Payne, K.J. (2009). *Simplicity Parenting: Using the extraordinary power of less to raise calmer, happier, and more secure kids.* New York: Ballantine Books.

Reggio Children (2001). *Making Learning Visible: Children as individual and group learners.* Reggio Emilia, Italy: Reggio Children.

Sahoo, D. (2012). Strategic change of campaign at Apple Inc. *From the Editor's Desk*, 5(2), 38–40.

Schwake, S. (2012). *Art Lab for Kids: 52 creative adventures in drawing, painting, printmaking, paper and mixed media for budding artists of all ages.* Bloomington, IN: Quarry Books.

Skibbe, L.E., Connor, C.M., Morrison, F.J. & Jewkes, A.M. (2011). Schooling effects on preschoolers' self-regulation, early literacy, and language growth. *Early Childhood Research Quarterly*, 26(1), 42–9.

Starke, P. (2013, May 3). Tech-savvy kids can't push a pencil. News Limited Network, www.news.com.au/technology/tech-savvy-kids-cant-push-a-pencil/story-e6frfro0–1226634952869 Accessed 23 June 2013.

Stavy, R. (ed.) (2012). *U-shaped Behavioral Growth.* New York: Elsevier.

Stone, M.K. (2009). *Smart by Nature: Schooling for sustainability.* Healdsburg, CA: Watershed Media.

Subrahmanyam, K., Greenfield, P., Kraut, R. & Gross, E. (2001). The impact of computer use on children's and adolescents' development. *Journal of Applied Developmental Psychology*, 22(1), 7–30.

Vaidhyanathan, S. (2011). Apple, demystified. *The Chronicle of Higher Education*, http://search.proquest.com/docview/900193019?accountid=13380 Accessed 3 March 2014.

Chapter 4

Digital media literacies in the early years

Michael Dezuanni and Sandra Gattenhof

Introduction

In the introduction to this book, we argued that a significant limitation within some approaches to teaching with iPads is the reliance on apps as 'educational software', where it is assumed children will learn through the 'transmission' of information and skills via these apps (Ito, 2009). One way that this is a significantly limited approach to the use of iPads in education is that this ignores the affordances of the iPad as a highly sophisticated device for creativity through media production. In this chapter, we provide examples of how the children we observed were able to use the iPads as a device for media production. We argue that it is not too far-fetched to claim that touch-screen devices with cameras and audio recording are a breakthrough technology for allowing young children to participate in multimodal communication in ways previously unavailable to them. Rather than simply being a consumption device, therefore, the iPad has clear potential as a media production device.

We frame our discussion through the lens of digital media literacies, drawing on the media education tradition to argue that this lower barrier to participation provides the opportunity for children to begin to learn about the digital cultures in which they live. This includes learning how to participate in digital culture through the development of conceptual understandings about the multimodal languages of the media, the purposes for making media and thinking about the audiences who use media. We argue that this is important learning for children whose media consumption occurs within global media cultures and in which media franchises are created that aim to appeal to children across a range of transmedia platforms. The toys children play with, the books they read, the digital games they play, the music they listen to and the apps they use are often linked across franchised concepts that form the basis for their play in digital culture (Marsh & Bishop, 2014).

Media education has often been put forward as a response to concerns about children's media use, although in recent years media education scholars have argued for the importance of recognising children's agency in media culture (Buckingham, 2003). In this chapter we draw on approaches to media education that recognise the need for children and young people to participate in both creative media production and critical discussion for the development of media literacies (Hoechsmann & Low, 2008). We contribute to the discussion within media education scholarship by arguing that to properly understand young children's development of digital media literacies, we need to account for the material and bodily aspects of their learning, not just their conceptual learning. We use a 'building blocks' model developed by Dezuanni, which outlines four 'building blocks' for assembling digital media literacies (Dezuanni, 2014). In the second part of the chapter we provide general observations of children's media production with the iPads and we then go on to discuss two examples of children's media production in more detail.

Children's media cultures

Young children living in high-tech communities in the second decade of the twenty-first century take part in global media cultures through viewing television, playing digital games and playing with toys that increasingly rely on cross-platform convergence and transmedia storytelling. Their experience is 'global' because so many of the products they use are distributed internationally by large international corporations like Sony, Apple, Microsoft, Google and Disney. A second tier of media distribution comes from national broadcasters such as the British Broadcasting Corporation (BBC), the Australian Broadcasting Corporation (ABC), The Public Broadcasting Service (PBS) in the United States and the Finnish Broadcasting Company (Yle), which often complement traditional distribution windows like television broadcasting and DVD sales with platforms such as Apple's App Store and Google Play to distribute online content. Children then interact with this content on touch-screen devices.

Cross-platform convergence and transmedia storytelling (Jenkins, 2006b) means that children often 'experience' a story concept as a media franchise across a range of devices, toys and publications. For instance, the BBC's television programme *In the Night Garden*, principally aimed at children aged 1 to 4, includes a 30-minute television programme that began airing in 2008 and as of 2014 is broadcast in 36 countries and 19 languages (DHX Media 2014); it is also accessible through internet television services such as BBC's iPlayer and Australia's ABC iView. There is an award-winning *In the Night Garden* interactive website (www.inthenightgarden.co.uk/); a range of toys commissioned by the show's production company DHX Media, such as plush toys, scooters, floor puzzles, play tents and inflatable seats. There is an *In the Night Garden* live entertainment theatre production that over 400,000 people have attended in the UK (www.nightgardenlive.com), a series of children's books published by Penguin Children's Books (DHX Media 2014) and an app available in Apple's iTunes App Store.

Young children's media experiences therefore extend beyond scheduled television viewing to include many aspects of their play, broader family life and the material culture they interact with in domestic spaces. Licensed media products provide the resources for a significant part of children's popular culture experiences, learning and identity formation (Nichols *et al.*, 2012). In a recent study of UK primary school children's schoolyard play, Rebekah Willett and colleagues (Willett *et al.*, 2013) demonstrate that the majority of children's play includes references to popular culture and media. Marsh and Richards (2013, p. 12) suggest:

> many children are located within a digital nexus in which play and creativity are central to multimodal, multimedia meaning-making practices . . . and in which particular media characters, texts and artefacts, seep into all aspects of their lives from a young age.

The prevalence of media culture in children's lives has long been the focus of community and social concern about the possible negative effects on children's learning, behaviour and social development (Gauntlett, 2005). Research by scholars such as Buckingham (2000) and Kinder (1991) suggests, however, that children are not powerless when using media and popular cultural resources and often use media for their own purposes to form their identities in unique ways. Jenkins (1992) and Ito (2010) suggest young people live in a participatory culture in which they use media resources to be creative, particularly in new media contexts where they have access to new technologies to make their own media through remixing and re-circulating media. One of the aims of this chapter is to discuss the extent to which such claims are valid for preschool-aged children.

Media education and digital media literacy

A key response to concerns about the relationship between young people and media has been the development of media education[1] in schools, which began as film appreciation in the 1930s in response to concerns about the effects of cinema attendance on children and young people (Bolas, 2009). Contemporary media education aims to enable young people to:

> interpret and make informed judgements as consumers of media; but it also enables them to become producers of media in their own right. Media education is about developing young people's critical *and* creative abilities.
>
> (Buckingham, 2003, p. 4 original emphasis)

The development of students' critical abilities typically involves analysis of media products and the contexts in which media are produced. Students learn to perform a range of tasks including analysis of the ways in which different media forms communicate through codes and conventions, for instance through the visual language of shot types, camera angles, editing techniques and use of sound and lighting. In more complex tasks, they learn to identify the layers of meaning that are potentially produced when audience members 'read' media products, by identifying how social and cultural norms are produced through the circulation of media products. Students also often consider the institutional contexts in which media products are created and how this relates to the purpose for their existence – for example to entertain, persuade, inform or educate. They might also consider the technological context in which media are produced and accessed/consumed and how the availability of different technologies impacts on the communication process. The development of creativity through media production in schools involves the use of communications technologies like cameras, sound recording equipment, computers and creative software for storytelling and exploring concepts. This includes the creation of narrative and non-narrative storytelling across the multiple contexts in which media and popular culture exist within society. Students develop skills to use production equipment and to follow organised production processes to design, produce and post-produce media products.

A central consideration for us in this chapter is the relationship between critical responses to media and creative production by preschool children. Obviously, many of the ways of being critical described above are unavailable to young children because they lack the frames of reference and metalanguage to discuss media in complex and abstract ways. Throughout our project, however, we saw children creatively using iPads to discuss their own and others' work and to think about how they could tell stories. Furthermore, the process of making media helped them develop understandings of how media can be used to communicate ideas. These processes may be more creative than critical, but we believe they opened up ways for the children to act upon the world and therefore to begin to develop agency in digitally mediated contexts. Later in the chapter, we will argue that the ways children learnt through media education in the preschool contexts was through a socio-material process that accounts for playful creativity with tools for communication and critical thinking associated with conceptual thinking.

A focus on the material aspects of media education in preschool contexts differs from established ways of thinking about media education, which tend to promote 'conceptual' thinking (Buckingham, 2013). In the late 1980s and early 1990s, the British Film Institute (BFI) developed an internationally influential set of media education curriculum categories – clusters of concepts – to be used with students in both primary and secondary schools in the UK (Bazalgette, 1992) which included: agency, category, technology, language, audience and representation to identify the types of learning that should take place within media education contexts. In this approach students produce and analyse media to develop knowledge through the key conceptual categories via the development of abstract thinking about media. For instance, they learn to understand how a film or television programme communicates by breaking it down into its component parts such as story structure, genre conventions and codes of communication – the shots, camera angles, editing, lighting and sound. Film and television texts are often deconstructed and made abstract in this way before students go ahead and recreate their own versions of television programmes. As we have suggested, this approach may not be suitable in preschool contexts where young children are less likely than older students to think abstractly. More fundamentally, though, a focus on the conceptual at the expense of the material/technological may fail to take account of important aspects of learning as students make media.

Another consideration for ways in which media education might continue to evolve is that digital technologies potentially change the relationship children and young people have with media. From one perspective, digital technologies add to the complexity of this relationship – because the means to media production and distribution is no longer concentrated in the hands of a small number of powerful producers such as film, television and news companies. As Lister *et al.* (2003) argue, the internet-connected computer is a powerful input/output device that allows an increasing number of people of all ages to create media content and distribute it. This is assisted by the convenience of online distribution platforms like YouTube and Facebook, but is also made possible through blogging, website production and podcasting. In this context, older media education questions about media ownership and bias are being usurped by new questions about social media ethics, the complexities of online behaviour and the new opportunities for transmedia production and distribution (Dezuanni & Ryan, 2014). These questions often still focus on the relationship between media, children and young people but they are new questions for new media forms. New technologies like internet-connected smartphones and tablet computers make it possible for more people than ever before to create rich multimodal media content to distribute to networks of friends and family and beyond. Every individual with access to these technologies is a potential media producer and distributer. Media production for media education is therefore no longer just focused on replicating industry-like media products, but is increasingly vernacular and used for everyday storytelling and communication (Dezuanni & Woods, 2014). There is the potential for media forms such as film and television to become less prominent in young people's lives as they spend increasing amounts of time playing digital games, watching internet video and curating their friends' media experiences by sharing, 'liking' and tagging on social media platforms (Potter, 2012). In these new digital contexts, the outcome of media education is not just 'media literacy' but may be more accurately described as 'digital media literacies'.

iPads, media production and digital media literacies

Our observations of young children's iPad use suggest touch-screen devices provide them with unprecedented opportunities to make and circulate media.

The iPad's touch-screen interface and simple menu systems enables even preschool children to become creative media producers; and this presents an opportunity for the development of digital media literacies in formal educational contexts. The iPad includes the apparatus to capture still and moving images, to record sound and to edit and mix images and sound using media production 'apps'. Throughout our project we saw children in all three preschool settings making media with the iPads; for instance through taking photographs and then combining these with audio recordings in an app like Book Creator. We observed production activity that very much resembled the kinds of learning that often takes place under the umbrella of media education in primary school settings. A key goal of this chapter, however, is to discuss the extent to which this production activity by 3- and 4-year-olds provides opportunities for student agency and engagement with conceptual understandings.

To get a sense of how iPads have changed the possibilities for media production with young children, it is worth recalling the procedure required to produce even simple media in the very recent past; or in the present, where production relies on non-touch screen technologies. For instance, prior to the arrival of tablet computers, video production involved gathering images using a digital still or video camera that was subsequently plugged into a computer using a USB lead. A keyboard and mouse was used to open software, which users then attempted to synch with the camera from which images were downloaded. The mouse was then used to drag and drop images into the software to re-arrange and edit them. Using the software required an understanding of complex menu systems, including multiple 'dropdown' menus, even in 'consumer' versions of software such as iMovie for the Macintosh computer. Similar processes were/are required even for simpler tasks such as taking digital still images to add to a PowerPoint presentation, or to make a simple poster that includes images and text. These processes of working with hardware, cables, files and folder systems and software can be challenging even for 8- and 9-year-old children (Dezuanni & Woods, 2014). They are certainly complex tasks for 3- and 4-year-olds. iPads simplify this process, resulting in a compromise in which creative potential and control over the final 'look' of a project is traded off against usability and accessibility. The iPad is a fully integrated device in which still images, audio and video footage is shot or recorded using the iPad and then stored in a directory that is inaccessible to the user, but which can be seamlessly accessed through multiple software apps. Once the digital materials are gathered, they are available within different apps and ready to be used. Software apps typically include only three or four menus, which means the full functionality of the software can be explored very quickly. In our project, children were very willing to explore these menus to see what was possible and they only occasionally became 'lost' within the app. In this sense, the iPad provides very low barriers to participation in media production – even for very young children. We are not claiming that children were somehow inherently able to use the apps and we note that quite intensive instruction and support from the teachers was required. As noted in other chapters in the book, however, the biggest challenge for children of this age was their inability to communicate through traditional print literacies; they much more easily communicated by using images and recorded sound created on the iPads.

The building blocks of digital media literacy

One of the questions we are most interested to explore through our consideration of media education with very young children is the extent to which conceptual thinking may begin to develop as students make media. As noted above, this is a key concern because media education aims to develop students' conceptual understandings about how media communicate and the social and cultural role media play in society. It is less likely in a kindergarten setting, though, than in contexts with older students, that substantive conversations about conceptual elements will take place. In addition, media scholars have increasingly argued that the development of digital media literacies relies on media production at least as much as media analysis (Buckingham, 2008; Jenkins, 2006a). Our observations of learning in the kindergarten context suggest that most 'critical' conversations occur as students make media rather than in isolated learning episodes with a specific focus on critical discussion. The 'building blocks' model of digital media literacy (Dezuanni, 2014) was developed after close observations of students learning through media production in a primary school context as part of a large four-year study of the relationship between digital technology and the development of traditional literacies.

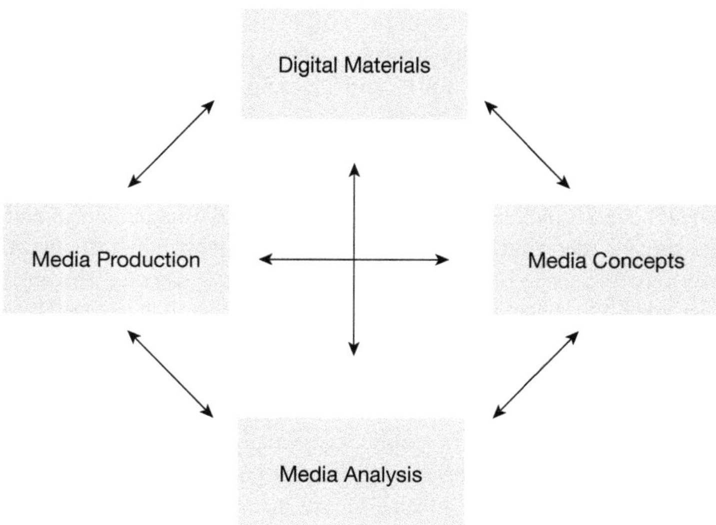

Figure 4.1 Building blocks for assembling digital media literacies

The current chapter argues that this model provides a means to understand how making media and developing conceptual understandings in preschool settings are intimately connected.

The building blocks of digital media literacy, as outlined in Figure 4.1, include *digital materials* and *media concepts* as knowledge domains and *media production* and *media analysis* as processes. Digital materials are the artefacts that are created and combined through media production, including still and moving images, recorded voice and sound effects, music, digital text and generated media (e.g. animations). Media concepts are the knowledge domains that outline how media communicate and the social, cultural and technological contexts in which communication takes place. Media production involves combining digital materials through editing, mixing and laying out into recognisable media products using available designs, including genre conventions. Media analysis involves 'deconstructing' existing media products to understand how they communicate and the meanings they generate in different contexts. It also includes taking part in meaningful conversations about different media forms' social and cultural roles. The building blocks approach is a socio-material model that recognises that individuals assemble and deploy digital media literacies both through physical interaction with technological tools within physical places and spaces and through the use of talk, conversation and spoken and written reflection.

The building blocks model suggests that both material and conceptual elements are necessary for the development of digital media literacies because media production involves physical processes such as holding and manipulating technological apparatuses like cameras, microphones, computer mouses and keyboards, in addition to thinking about how particular shot sizes, layouts, audio levels and lighting techniques will help to convey messages. For instance, it is impossible for a student to communicate a visual message using different shot types if they do not know how to hold and manipulate a camera. While they might understand the difference between different types of shots, if they cannot create their own images to communicate, they will not have the opportunity to employ digital literacy skills and knowledge. Digital media literacy therefore involves bodily knowledge associated with competence in effectively using technological tools. Other bodily knowledge is also important. For instance, knowing how to choreograph one's own body in a spatial relationship to an object to take a photograph of an object or to effectively record a sound takes practice and bodily control, particularly when looking at the world through a camera viewfinder or the screen on an iPad; and this is particularly challenging for young children. On the other hand, of course, without the conceptual knowledge to tell a story or explore ideas, technical competence has significant limitations. In the sections that follow, we aim to illustrate that when the material and conceptual elements of digital media literacies effectively come together, young children are able to participate as producers of media content in digital culture as media producers and storytellers, not just as consumers.

The iPad as a device for media production

Our project demonstrates that the iPad is a sophisticated media production device that 3- and 4-year-old children can use to be creative and to communicate. Across all three sites, the vast majority of children had very little difficulty turning on the iPads or accessing the apps. In the few cases where children had not previously operated an iPad or iPhone, they seemed to very quickly learn to use the on/off switch, the touch-screen interface to access the apps and the 'home' button to exit an app or return to the 'home' screen. Almost all children also very readily used the volume buttons to increase and decrease the sound levels on the device. We also noted that once the children were shown how to record a digital image or video with the iPads, most were easily able to undertake this task, although some children struggled to physically hold and stretch their finger across the iPad to the on-screen button to record an image. As a result, one of the teachers suggested that the smaller iPad mini would be more easily used by children of this age to take photographs. A significant positive aspect of using the iPads for image capture was that the whole iPad screen acts as a viewfinder and it is easy for the children to see what they are recording. Young children often struggle to use the viewfinder on a traditional camera. Most children also very quickly learnt to use drawing and painting apps like Brushes and enjoyed tracing their fingers across the iPad screen to make digital 'marks'. The children also readily learnt to record their own voices using a 'record' button within specific apps like Draw and Tell, and Book Creator.

Our observations suggest that the iPad's touch-screen interface enables 3- and 4-year-olds to draw and paint and to record images and sound with

Figure 4.2 A Preschool child using the iPad to record images

little difficulty. It was more challenging for the children to use apps to arrange their photographs/images and combine them with audio recordings. Most children required initial one-on-one assistance to use an app like Book Creator to import their images and then arrange them on the page through a 'drag and drop' process. Likewise, using the menu system within each different app to change background colours or the colour of their 'paintbrush' required quite a lot of initial assistance. The menu systems in iPad apps are generally much simpler to use than menu systems in software designed for desktop and laptop computers. For instance, most apps for creative production have only three or four menu buttons, typically including: an image button to allow the user to import a photo or movie; a text button that allows the user to access the virtual keyboard to enter text and to change the font colour and size; a microphone or sound recording button to record voice or sound effects; a 'cog wheel' or 'inspector' button that allows the user to change settings such as the background colour of a page; and a 'send' or 'publish' button to share the product in a variety of ways. Although these menu systems were quite daunting at first for the children we observed, once these skills were mastered the majority were very

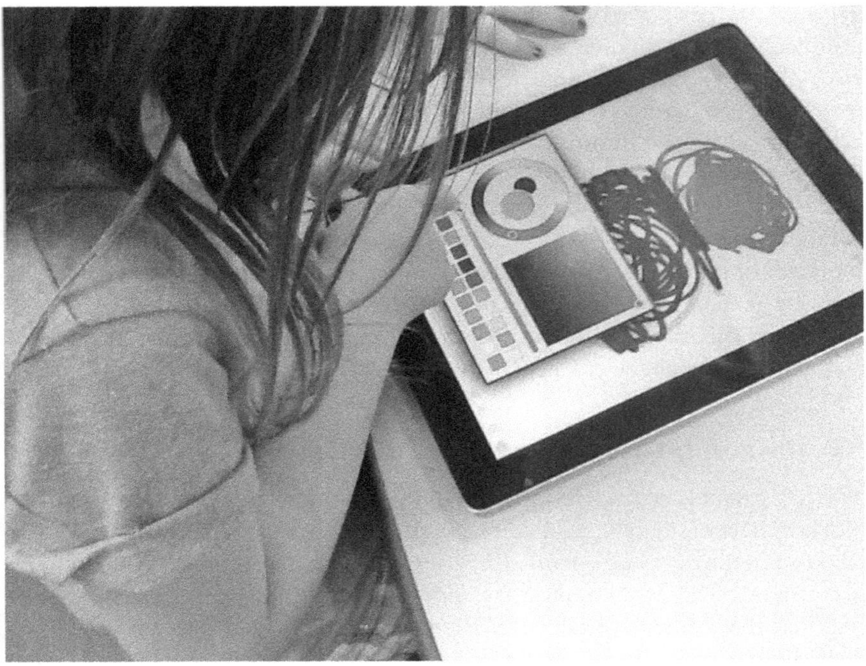

Figure 4.3 A preschool child using the menu system on the app Brushes to choose different brush colours

Source: Brushes app: free.libre open source software

Reprinted by permission of QUT Legal

willing to experiment with the apps to communicate and be creative. Some apps, such as Draw and Tell (Duck Duck Moose, 2013) were also designed specifically for children and so the menu systems were 'inviting' rather than obstructive for children of this age.

The main difficulties with using the iPads for media production with the children were to do with the challenges of allowing the children to take them from the flat surface of a table to carry them around the centre, including outdoors, to record images. The teachers were initially concerned about the fragility of the iPads and most centres purchased some form of cover or 'big grip' frame to make it easier for the children to hold the iPads and to provide some protection in the event that they were dropped. As it eventuated, only 1 of 30 iPads across the three centres was damaged during the project and this was an accident involving a teacher rather than a student. Despite this, the teachers agreed that, particularly at the beginning of the project, they were hesitant to allow the children to walk around with the iPads on a regular basis and, in this respect, the children were only occasionally allowed to experiment with image capture.

Another challenge was recording sound. The teachers all drew attention to the difficulties of recording sound due to the amount of noise the children generated as they played and involved themselves in various activities. This made it difficult for the children to record their voices on apps and this often led to poor-quality sound recordings where it was difficult to hear what the children recorded. The teachers sometimes allowed the children to use a quiet space – like their office – to record their voices, but this was not always practical. The final frustration was the difficulty of sharing the students' work. For instance, while each early childhood centre had success with the app Book Creator for combining images, text and sound, they all pointed to the difficulty of sharing the electronic publication file (.epub), as parents and carers required special software to be able to read the epubs. Some apps restrict publication to 'the cloud' and others do not allow projects to be easily printed. More will be said about these challenges in Chapter 8.

Re-designing the playground

The first example of student production we want to explore using the building blocks model of digital media literacy is students' use of the app Draw and Tell to communicate their plans for improving the Outer North Centre's playground. This is an appropriate project to explore the model because it required the students to take digital images, import these into the app, draw over the top of the image and then record their voice to explain the design. The project required students to create and combine different digital materials (a still image, drawing and voice recording) through a production process. It also required them to develop conceptual understandings such as appropriate shot size and type, storytelling through explaining the design and analysis as

Figure 4.4 Emily's design for the playground using Draw and Tell
Source: Copyright Duck Duck Moose
Reprinted by permission of Duck Duck Moose

they viewed other students' designs and commented on them. While the outcome was not a generic media product intended to entertain or inform (it was more design-based) it involved key aspects of media production and therefore the development of digital media literacies.

To complete this task, Emily (pseudonym) recorded a still image of part of the garden using a medium shot. This was achieved after assistance from her teacher, who had outlined the task for the students and then worked with each individual child to help them frame up an image and record it. This included a discussion of the most appropriate type of shot to take to allow it to be drawn on. Emily opened the app Draw and Tell, imported her image and then drew over the top of the image to outline her designs. From left to right in Figure 4.4 we see her representations of a flower, a cubby house with a ladder, what appears to be a decoration on a plant and a fairy. In the final step, Emily used the voice record button to record her voice over the image while she moved her finger on the screen, pointing to each part of the design. The smudgy 'spot' in the middle of Figure 4.4 represents where Emily had placed her finger on the design as she spoke about her cubby house concept. As she traced her finger over the screen she recorded the following:

> I want, umm, a flower and a . . . cubby house and a really spikey thing on the bush and a fairy (20 seconds).

The outcome of this process is the creation of a 20-second movie file that is saved to the iPad's camera role (as a.mov file), which can then be shared with other students, teachers, parents and caregivers. As Emily undertakes this process of multimodal communication she is developing complex literacies as she works across modes to share her ideas as part of the process of beginning to develop digital media literacies. The building blocks framework helps us to understand Emily's learning because using technologies to communicate is not just a matter of using different language systems (visual, spoken, alphabetic) for different social and cultural purposes. It also involves material/bodily processes, a production process that includes specific stages and an ability to appropriately combine digital materials using software (Dezuanni, 2014). Part of the outcome of this overall process is that students begin to learn how media is produced through processes of selection and construction.

Media production with an iPad is material and bodily because recording a usable image requires the child/producer to hold the iPad still to appropriately frame and record the image. The iPad is a technological apparatus that becomes an extension of what the child can see without the camera and then through the screen, and how they are spatially located in relationship with their subject. The process of recording a medium shot of the garden is not just a process of framing the image correctly, which requires conceptual understanding, it also involves knowing how to hold your body still and to recognise the weight and 'feel' of the iPad in your hands. In this sense, media production combines the material and conceptual. Conceptually, it also involves knowing how to interpret the technological representation of the subject on the screen/viewfinder and the relationship of this to 'reality'. Materially, it requires bodily learning or what Hayles (1999) refers to as incorporation, which is the process of the body learning to use an apparatus as a natural extension of the body. This conceptual and material work continues as Emily undertakes work on her production through several steps. She physically interacts with the iPad to conceptually represent her ideas by adding layers of digital material to the production to make a final product. Bringing the conceptual and material together is not a straightforward process for 3- and 4-year-olds and Emily was assisted with each of the steps with one-on-one assistance from her teacher. The outcome, though, is an important step for Emily toward learning to use technology for representational processes and to develop digital media literacies.

The photography project

The second example of media production we wish to explore using the building blocks model of digital media literacy is an iPad photography project that took place at the South Side Centre. The centre director initiated this project when she realised that the iPads would allow her to fulfil a long-term ambition to introduce photography to the children. She explained that she had not previously allowed children to use the centre's one camera although she was aware that other centres often allowed children to take photos. She explained that while she believed the children were competent and capable with technology, her previous lack of access to the technology and her own lack of confidence ruled it out. She was excited, though, to have access to the camera on the iPads:

> Oh these iPads have got cameras on, yes! I'm fine with them having the camera now so it's that confidence in, you know, letting go and being able to let them use it and know that they can use it and they'll show you things about it that you didn't know. Yeah so that's the learning curve for me.

Moving from having access to just one digital camera to suddenly having access to ten made a significant difference to the teacher's willingness to let the children experiment with digital photography. It is also worth noting that in one of the first professional development sessions the teachers undertook during the project, they learnt how to record digital still and video footage with the iPads and how to arrange images using different apps like Book Creator. It is likely that the teacher's confidence to try photography with the students resulted from both access to the technology and new knowledge about ways to use photography and apps with the students. It is also very notable that the teacher defers to her students' abilities and knowledge of technology. Her experimentation in the project has paid off in the sense that she now has the confidence to allow the students to experiment with image creation and manipulation. The resulting pedagogy emphasises that learning with the technology is largely exploratory and that once the students have been shown some basics they are able to experiment and show each other and the teacher how to achieve particular results with the camera and the apps.

The teacher described how she taught the group about wide, medium and close-up shots, explaining that close-up shots often result in abstract images. She emphasised, though, that intentional or direct teaching about this was quite minimal with only a brief overview during group time:

> I mean that was as much as I said to them . . . that when we do some photography I'd like you to have a look at what things look like from a long way away. And then when they get up close, and then really close so you can't really tell what it is.

Despite the simplicity of this explanation, the teacher's focus on ways of seeing through the screen goes beyond an explanation of the simple framing of images. Rather, she draws attention to the concept of how objects can be represented through photography, particularly how processes of selection and construction can change an audience's perception of an object. The teacher provides the students with a purpose for their photography that emphasises a conceptual understanding of image production. Each resulting image is an example of digital material that helps to tell the story of an object, which we see in its broader spatial context (the wide shot); at a 'natural' distance (medium shot); and as an abstraction (extreme close-up). Of course, these spatial arrangements are central to the language of visual communication and form the basis for how a range of print, broadcast and interactive media communicate. Film, television, advertising, news reporting and video games all rely on the sequential arrangement of different shot types. This form of communication is not just conceptual, however, because the production of these images relies on the choreography of the camera in relation to the object. To record different types of shots, the photographer/filmmaker needs to physically move their body and the camera to be in the right spatial proximity to the object. This is something young children need to be carefully shown. At first, the teacher sometimes had to physically move the children backward and forward to show them how to appropriately choreograph their shot. Again, this points to the conceptual and material components of digital media literacy.

The teacher was surprised at the sophistication of some of the images the children created in the preschool and the extent to which the students engaged with the project, even at home. The children were allowed to borrow an iPad to take home to use and the teacher sometimes set optional homework activities for the students. This included a repetition of the photography project where the children were encouraged to take images at home and parents were informed by the South Side teacher about the process of taking images 'from a distance,

Figure 4.5 Preschool child's wide, medium and close-up shot, recorded on an iPad at home

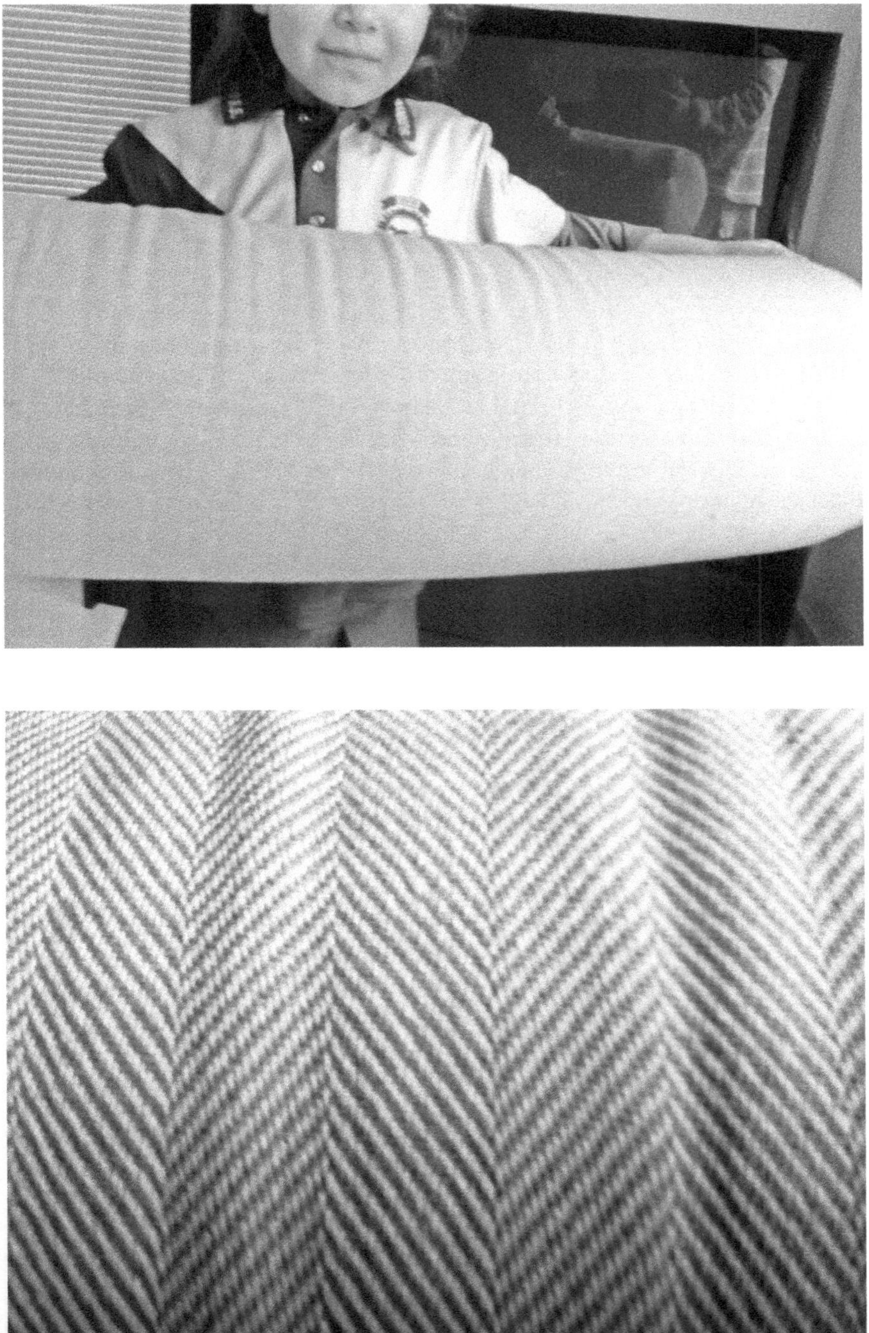

Figure 4.5 *continued*

a little bit closer and then up close and looking at textures'. In this manner, the work the children undertook in the preschool was rehearsed by some of them at home. The children then returned the work to share proudly, often surprising the teachers:

> some of the photography that we've got back has been outstanding . . . one child has a log in her lounge room, like a log-shaped pillow. And the texture on that up close! Yeah I was really surprised when the third photo came on and went wow look at that.

Many of the children's iPad camera rolls had similar sequences of images, although the close-up shots were sometimes out of focus due to the children's limited knowledge about the iPad's inability to adjust to macro mode. It is evident that most of the students have developed an understanding of the difference between shot types and have been able to materially produce different types of images with the iPads. In this sense, the students have developed fundamental knowledge for the development of digital media literacies about sequencing images and the fundamentals of storytelling. The 'wow' factor the teacher refers to in relation to the log-shaped pillow close-up likely results from the teachers' surprise that children of this age are capable of thinking abstractly about images and having the skill to reproduce a specific image. It is impossible to know how intentional this image is in the sense that the crisp focus of the image and the already abstract pattern on the pillow could arguably have led to a 'happy accident' where abstraction is even more pronounced than intended by the child. Even if this is the case, though, it is clear that the child intended to take a sequence of images following her teacher's instruction and this has led to the development of new knowledge. The final product is not as important to learning as the process the student has undertaken.

Beyond developing an understanding of shot types and sequencing, the children also developed knowledge of the production process and the process of using software to change and combine images to communicate to an audience. The teacher was pleased with the extent to which the children demonstrated the ability to use the iPads to record images and then use them for different purposes:

> the cameras have been great and to be able to document their own work and then be able to use that in another app. They know how to, they know where the pictures are, they know where to find them. For any of the apps that say you can access the pictures they know how to go and get it. So they've learnt a lot in that respect so the camera has been awesome.

An important aspect of developing digital media literacies is the ability to use and combine digital materials for different purposes through different production processes (Dezuanni, 2014). It is informative that the teacher indicates that the children are able to recognise the 'picture' icon in different apps and understand that they can access the images they have recorded to import them into the app and then use them in different ways. Again, this seems to reinforce our argument that iPads lower the barrier to participation in media production for young children. It is not too far-fetched to claim that the iPad provides children of this age with the first genuine opportunity to communicate with media technologies in ways that no previous technology has. We are not claiming that the iPad is somehow emancipatory. Clearly, children need a great deal of one-on-one support to learn how to use the iPad and specific apps and, more importantly, they need to be provided with opportunities to develop specific conceptual and material knowledge about how to undertake media production. What we have shown in these examples is that when 3- and 4-year-old children are provided with opportunities to create their own work using the iPad, the device is a sophisticated media production system that the children can operate. The barrier to participation is no longer the technology but the conceptual and material learning opportunities made available to the children.

Conclusion

We began this chapter by discussing the complex digital media cultures in which young children live in today's global media ecologies. iPad use is just one activity children undertake as they consume media, often as part of the broader experience of a media 'franchise'. For instance, the Lego company has been particularly successful in creating and using media franchise concepts as it has moved from a company focused on providing coloured building blocks to a broader media company that licenses television shows, comics, books and creates building sets featuring established movie concepts like Harry Potter and Marvel super heroes. Using a Lego app or playing the Lego Harry Potter game on the iPad invites a child into a whole play-based system in which they can consume 'Harry Potter' in multiple ways. Media education scholarship (Ito, 2010; Marsh, 2005; Potter, 2012) has argued that children have complex relationships with media concepts in which they enter complex negotiations around meaning-making, identity formation and learning. In this context, one role of media education is to help children to understand how media products are made, how stories are created within specific products and across transmedia systems. Media education can help children to 'talk back' to media concepts by taking part in conversations about media and by producing their own media that makes media construction explicit.

Before we began this project, we were unsure if young children would be able to use the iPads for media production and therefore enter into the kinds of complex 'conversations' with media called for by media education scholarship. Observations throughout the project, however, suggest that 3- and 4-year-olds are very capable of using iPads and apps for media production. We are not claiming that this alone will lead to the development of complex digital media literacies; this is a process that will likely occur over several years when children and young people are given opportunities to engage in creative media production and critically reflective consumption through media education. It is our belief, though, that creative production using the iPads can assist young children to begin to navigate the complex media worlds in which they live on a daily basis. The iPad provides the apparatus to allow this to occur and the challenge for teachers is to find ways to assist children to understand how stories are constructed, how sequences of images begin to create meaning and how different digital materials can be combined to add layers of meaning and complexity to a media product. The examples provided in this chapter present the beginnings of what this kind of work might look like with very young children.

Note

1 In the United States and Canada, 'media literacy' is often used rather than media education. Media education is more commonly used in the United Kingdom, Australia and New Zealand.

References

Bazalgette, C. (1992). Key aspects of media education. In M. Alvarado & O. Boyd-Barrett (eds), *Media Education: An introduction*. London: British Film Institute.

Bolas, T. (2009). *Screen Education: From film appreciation to media studies*. Bristol, UK: Intellect.

Buckingham, D. (2000). *After the Death of Childhood: Growing up in the age of electronic media*. Cambridge: Polity Press.

—— (2003). *Media Education: Literacy, learning and contemporary culture*. Cambridge: Polity Press.

—— (2008). Defining digital literacies: What do young people need to know about digital media? In C. Lankshear & M. Knobel (eds), *Digital Literacies: Concepts, policies and practices* (pp. 71–89). New York: Peter Lang.

—— (2013). Challenging concepts: Learning in the media classroom. In P. Fraser & J. Wardle (eds), *Current Perspectives in Media Education: Beyond the manifesto* (pp. 24–40). London: Palgrave.

Dezuanni, M.L. (2014). The building blocks of digital media literacy: socio-material participation and the production of media knowledge. *Journal of Curriculum Studies*. DOI: 10.1080100220272.2014.966152

Dezuanni, M.L. & Ryan, M.D. (2014). Next generation filmmaking and media arts in the Australian curriculum. *Media Education Research Journal*, 4(2), 33–45.

Dezuanni, M.L. & Woods, A.F. (2014). Developing media production skills for literacy in a primary school classroom: Digital materials, embodied knowledge and material contexts. In G. Barton (ed.), *Literacy in the Arts: Retheorising learning and teaching* (pp. 143–60). Switzerland: Springer.

DHX Media (2014, January 22). Media Release. www.dhxmedia.com/press-room/473-dhx-media-appoints-cplg-to-represent-in-the-night-garden-in-the-uk.html

Duck Duck Moose (2013). Draw and Tell. Duck Duck Moose. www.duckduckmoose.com/
Gauntlett, D. (2005). *Moving Experiences: Media effects and beyond.* Eastleigh: John Libby Publishing.
Hayles, N.K. (1999). *How We Became Posthuman: Virtual bodies in cybernetics, literature, and informatics.* Chicago, IL: University of Chicago Press.
Hoechsmann, M. & Low, B.E. (2008). *Reading Youth Writing: 'New' literacies, cultural studies & education.* New York: Peter Lang.
Ito, M. (2009). *Engineering Play: A cultural history of children's software.* Cambridge, MA: MIT Press.
—— (2010). *Hanging Out, Messing Around, and Geeking Out: Kids living and learning with new media.* Cambridge, MA: MIT Press.
Jenkins, H. (1992). *Textual Poachers, Television Fans and Participatory Culture.* New York: Routledge.
Jenkins, H. (2006a). *Confronting the Challenges of Participatory Culture: Media education for the 21st century.* Chicago, IL: The MacArthur Foundation.
Jenkins, H. (2006b). *Convergence Culture: Where old and new media collide.* New York: New York University Press.
Kinder, M. (1991). *Playing with Power in Movies, Television and Video Games: From Muppet babies to teenage mutant ninja turtles.* Berkeley, CA: University of California Press.
Lister, M., Dovey, J., Giddings, S., Grant, I. & Kelly, K. (2003). *New Media: A critical introduction.* London: Routledge.
Marsh, J. (2005). *Popular Culture, New Media and Digital Literacy in Early Childhood.* London; New York: RoutledgeFalmer.
Marsh, J. & Bishop, J.C. (2014). *Changing Play: Play, media and commercial culture from the 1950s to the present day.* Maidenhead: Open University Press.
Marsh, J. & Richards, C. (2013). Play, Media and Children's Playground Cultures. In R. Willett, C. Richards, J. Marsh, A. Burn & J.C. Bishop (eds), *Children, Media and Playground Cultures: Ethnographic studies of school playtimes.* London: Palgrave.
Nichols, S., Rowsell, J., Nixon, H. & Rainbird, S. (2012). *Resourcing Early Learners: New networks, new actors.* New York: Routledge.
Potter, J. (2012). *Digital Media and Learner Identity: The new curatorship.* New York: Macmillan.
Willett, R., Richards, C., Marsh, J., Burn, A. & Bishop, J.C. (2013). *Children, Media and Playground Cultures: Ethnographic studies of school playtime.* London: Palgrave Macmillan.

Chapter 5

Drama, storymaking and iPads in the early years

Sandra Gattenhof and Michael Dezuanni

Introduction

No matter if we are young or old it is part of the human impulse to create and tell stories about our experiences, to make sense of each moment by placing it within larger narratives. It has been said that 'narrative is the primary form through which we understand and give meaning to our experience' (Polkinghorne, 1988). Young children are drawn to recounting their life moments through dramatic play, oral re-telling and image to share their experiences with others, to construct a sense of identity and to make meaning of the world.

Today's mobile devices, such as iPads, 'are equipped with media-capture tools that can be used to create multimodal stories from anything that children experience, imagine and want to share' (Bonsignore *et al.*, 2013, p. 4). The majority of the research and commentary available to date about mobile digital devices and storytelling has been focused upon interactive games, simulations and interactive fiction. There is very little discussion about the possible application of mobile digital devices to support storytelling by young children or the possible enhancement of early literacy skill acquisition through storymaking and storytelling.

In this chapter we consider how the iPad and selected applications such as Draw and Tell (Duck Duck Moose, 2013), Popplet (Notion, 2013) and Puppet Pals (Polished Play LLC, 2013) can assist children in collaborative storying, re-telling and sequencing story moments that can assist young children in their acquisition of oracy and their understanding of the world, both real and imagined, and their personal relationships. The data gathered from the project will also be analysed through the lens of 'critical and creative thinking' (ACARA, 2013, pp. 20–21) skills articulated as one of the general capabilities required in all subject areas of the Australian national curriculum, but which has particular application to the arts subject areas. In this chapter, we consider artefacts created by preschool children using iPads and selected apps, and interviews conducted with preschool children and their caregivers during our research project. We then offer examples of practice to assist preschool teachers in supporting children in their storymaking using the iPad and discuss approaches for engagement that twins the live and mediatised representation of a story.

Storytelling, dramatic play and lifeworlds of preschool children

Storytelling is an important developmental experience for young children. It is the first form of narrative literature they can fully understand and in which they can participate. There are several types of stories to tell; the easiest for the preschool child is the traditional oral tale drawn from the annals of folktales and fairy tales. There are also stories of personal experience and imagined stories. 'Storytelling of all sorts is the primary form through which we understand and impose order on our experience' (Cassell & Ryokai, 2001, p. 2). Storytelling is a social experience with oral narrative, incorporating linguistic features that display a 'sophistication that goes beyond the level of conversation' (Mallan, 1991, p. 14). The efficacy of combining apps that enable child-centred storytelling on the iPad to develop multimodal literacy in preschool-aged children has been explored in depth in Chapter 1, therefore this chapter will take the position that storytelling is a 'literacy event' (Heath, 1982, p. 50) as discussed in Chapter 1.

At this juncture it is important to define the nature of storytelling as it applies to the lifeworlds of preschool children. Mallan describes storytelling as 'using oral language in a social context to relate something heard, read, witnessed, dreamt or experienced' (Mallan, 1991, p. 5). With storytelling, Mallan says, 'the interaction is creative, as both the teller and listener create the story' (ibid.). Storytelling is interactional in that it depends on the use of facial expressions, vocal qualities and bodily gesture to convey meaning. Mallan also defines the differentiated nature of storytelling and story reading; '[s]torytelling is born out of an oral tradition; story reading depends on the written text' (Mallan, 1991, p. 5). The common thread that draws these two story forms together is that of the child's imagination. It is through the imagination that innovation solutions have been found to local and global problems both large and small, so the nurturing of the imagination cannot be underestimated (Robinson, 2011). As Mallan (1991) articulates, 'exercising their imaginations is an important stage in the development of higher level thinking skills (p. 10). No matter what form the sharing of life experience or imagined events take, '[s]tory enables children to give shape to their life experiences through recounting them, or to compare them with similar experiences from literary sources' (Mallan, 1991, p. 12).

It is important to provide a caveat about the use of the term drama in this chapter. Strictly speaking the preschool children in the project did not participate in activities associated with dramatic form through interaction with the iPad. This is because drama is essentially an embodied art form, that is, an art form in which a child explores their world through the body and through language and the voice. The apps used in the project did not have the similar capacities to those that are available through online games and console games in which lifelike action and dialogue can be replicated. However, the apps used for the activities undertaken by the children such as Draw and Tell, Popplet and Puppet Pals, possess capacities associated with dramatic form that can be captured under the concepts of storytelling and storymaking. Storytelling sits in an arc of practice that is aligned to dramatic play. 'Dramatic play is generally viewed, by those who see themselves as drama practitioners and theorists, as being a member of the "symbolic order of drama"' (Dunn, 2003, p. 119). The features common to both dramatic play and storytelling is that both activities can be child-initiated; are centred around the communication of experience that can be both real and imagined; they are playful and experimental; engage social interaction and they are focused on '. . . sense-making . . . in time and space, and find cause and effect – storytelling – shaping for ourselves the ongoing personal narrative and shaping with others the social narratives of our lives' (O'Toole, 2009, p. 4).

In drama education circles, careful attention is paid to the need to strike a balance between child-initiated play and teacher/adult play when structuring drama experiences. Likewise, this principle should be applied to storytelling episodes so that preschool children have the opportunity to make and tell stories both independently of adult intervention and in an environment of co-construction with peers or adults. According to Trousdale (1990) '[s]torytelling offers ways to bring children into the act of storymaking, ways of creating stories with children and not just *for* or *to* children' (p. 164, original emphasis). The following section demonstrates how the apps Draw and Tell and Puppet Pals support independent story construction prior to sharing and how Popplet allows a child to make independent choices in building a story within an adult-supported environment. Prior to beginning the exploration of the app and their storytelling capacities it is important to define the nature of storytelling in a preschool learning environment.

Storymaking, story sharing and oral language development

There is a wealth of documented research that supports the link between arts engagement, in which storymaking can sit, and literacy development (see Caldwell & Vaughan, 2012; Deasy, 2002; Ewing, 2010; Fiske, 1999; Hetland & Winner, 2001; O'Toole, 1991). O'Toole and Stinson (2013) point out that 'in the political rhetoric and the dominant curricula, "literacy" still almost invariably means the ability to master written text and also occasionally computer technology' (p. 159). Our conception of literacy in this chapter is an expanded one that includes multimodal forms, particularly oral and visual literacy. Hetland and Winner (2001) undertook a meta-analysis of 80 reports on the impact of the arts on student achievement and 'identifed a causal link between classroom drama and increased verbal skills, which transferred into new materials' (p. 74). As stated previously in this chapter, the preschool students were not involved in what could be strictly classified as drama activities; however, as drama has a strong oral component to its participation and reception by children, Hetland and Winner's finding can easily be applied to storymaking events. Mallan (1991) notes in her research that:

> When children are engaged in the social function of storytelling they are learning to listen, to participate in and to understand story language or narrative discourse. These three skills are important in assisting children with the mechanics of reading and writing, which are not to be seen as ends in themselves, but as pathways to the more sophisticated use of language in everyday life.
>
> (Mallan, 1991, p. 13)

On the other side of this argument, some researchers (Christakis *et al.*, 2009; O'Toole and Stinson, 2013; Ward, 2004) state that engagement in screen-based technologies has a detrimental effect on the oracy development in the contemporary generation of young children. In this chapter we seek to offer a position that marks out a site in which the interface between human face-to-face storymaking and the benefits that come from these social interactions such as fluency, vocabulary, understanding of language registers, abstract thinking and expressive language (O'Toole and Stinson, 2013, p. 160) may take place within a mediatised environment. This is an idea we will explore in greater depth later in this chapter.

Using apps for storymaking and to create a representation of self and others

For the remainder of the chapter, we are going to adopt the use of the term storymaking rather than storytelling to represent the type of drama-based activity that was engaged in by and with the preschool children, their teachers and their caregivers. The reason for the use of storymaking is that it denotes a more active engagement from both the teller (maker) and the listener. Wynne-Willson (2014) articulates the position of storymaking in the world of the child by saying that:

> The process of story-making is a really golden activity, for a number of reasons. . . . [T]heir role as exercise for the imagination muscle, and food for the soul, the place of stories perched between reality and imagination. When the stories are springing new from children as we go, one of the beauties of that process is that there are no right answers.
>
> (para. 5)

Use of the term storymaking supports Dewey's position (1934) that both children and adults do not learn merely by having an experience, but the learning occurs in the reflection on the experience – in this case the discussion of the story idea, themes and characters with child peers and adults. By making storytelling a collaborative and co-constructed event 'we can help children feel comfortable enough in storytelling to be confident of their own emergent narrative ability, to take risks, to elaborate, to invent, to explore, and thereby grow' (Trousdale, 1990, p. 173). It also allows for a more accurate representation of the physical engagement with the iPad by the child when constructing a story for sharing with an app.

Storymaking through dramatic play is an activity that most children do instinctively. They re-enact real events and play out imaginative ones. 'The origins of plays and playing are one and the same. For very young children, role play and acting out are one of the key ways of making sense of the world' (Wynne-Willson, 2014, para. 7). Drama and the embedded genre of storymaking are child-centred activities. The impetus for action can derive from the direct experience of the child and can be transferred to the 'outer world of objects and events, rather than the other way around' (McLeod, 1988, p. 10). In the recent past, however, the digital resources for young children to make stories have not been available. For instance, Cassell and Ryokai's research in the late 1990s argued:

> interactive storytelling available commercially for children was limited to applications that read storybook stories to children, software that provided sample first sentences for child writers, or authoring environments that allowed children to choose from sets of predefined characters and predefined text to make up plays.
>
> (Cassell & Ryokai, 2001, p. 4)

The iPad has made available a cornucopia of apps that not only allow children to read and interact with digital books (Reading Eggs, for example) but also allow preschool children, both independently and with adult support, to construct multimodal story representations for sharing with their peers, their preschool teachers and their caregivers (see Chapters 1 and 4). With the acknowledgement that 'mobile technologies are integral components in children's daily lives and possess unique affordances for learning and self-expression (Bonsignore *et al.*, 2013, p. 4), let us take some time to look at each of some apps individually to understand how each provides a platform for storymaking. The discussion focuses on one app that produces static products (Popplet) and two apps that create interactive output (Draw and Tell; Puppet Pals). The section also outlines the differences in the apps that require adult support and the app that can be used more independently by a preschool child once they have been provided with instruction on the icons, buttons and options.

Storymaking with Draw and Tell

As articulated in Chapter 2, one of the three key principles for the inclusion of iPads in preschool setting is that quality learning requires intervention and redirection by adults. This principle can be broadly captured under the process of scaffolding for learning in which specialised instructional support, provided by a caregiver or preschool teacher, need to be in put in place to best facilitate learning. In the realm of storymaking the adult acts as companion in the co-construction of meaning. The ultimate act of meaning-making occurs once the story is shared with an audience, the child's peers or adult supporters. The co-construction develops physical and emotional bonds that enhance the literacy event. 'Besides the words and the events in the stories, children need just as much the emotional connection with those around them' (Miscov, 2014, para. 3) for the effectiveness of the storymaking to be impactful in terms of sense-making in the life experience of a preschool child. Draw and Tell in its simplest terms embodies the title of the app. Preschool children are able to draw an image using a variety of crayons, brushes and pencils. There are also stickers that the children can add to their image and stencils that can be used. All the visual art materials are indicated with easily recognised icons. Once the child has completed their image, the app allows the child to touch a record button to tell the story of the image. Both the image and voice recording can then be saved and replayed as many times as the child may wish to share it. The following interview vignette demonstrates how a parent of one preschool child in the project found great pleasure in sharing his child's storymaking process.

Vignette 1

P = parent
I = Interviewer (QUT Researcher)

I: Did you always work on the iPad with the children or did they use it alone?
P: I was always in the vicinity but they were, they did have times where they were just sitting using it on their own. And then there were times well for example the . . . Draw and Tell, is that the one where they tell the story and it plays back their words? So he would sort of start that activity and I might wander off for a little bit and then come back and see what he was doing. . . . I was trying to encourage him to do the creative ones because I could see the value. But he did enjoy making his own story and talking about how he had a good imagination with that.
I: And did you find that enriching in terms of what you were listening to?
P: Yes it was lovely. Yeah and my son got a lot of joy listening to it back, hearing his own version of events. That was a lovely app. I really enjoyed that app very much.

Through the process of storymaking using Draw and Tell and children's subsequent sharing of their stories with adults, such as their caregivers and preschools teachers, adults 'make important discoveries about the behaviour of their own child, his interests, his relation to others, how the child communicates'

(Miscov, 2014, para. 16). As outlined earlier in this chapter, the nature of storymaking is interactional and it is not so much the sharing of the story that has instrumental value but it is the social aspect of the literacy event in which meaning-making occurs. As a corollary to this, 'when storytelling is combined with judicious questioning and re-telling strategies, comprehension skills at the literal, inferential and critical levels can be developed (Dwyer in Mallan, 1991, p. 13). While the app Draw and Tell somewhat privileges the visual elements in the storymaking event, it does contain a strong oral component that is key in storymaking and oral literacy development and in the development of multimodal story forms.

The vignette also demonstrates the usability of the Draw and Tell app. Initially the preschool teachers demonstrated the app to individuals or small groups as part of daily activities in which the iPad was a choice at one of the activity centres in the preschool room. Once the child recognised the icons for the visual art materials to construct their image and how to record their story, they could use Draw and Tell with some independence. Adult intervention was required to save the story for future sharing in the iPad's photo album. Draw and Tell can be used to make stories based in real or imagined events providing great flexibility in the preschool learning experience. The app allows children – with minimal intervention from adults – to both illustrate and vocalise a story that can be shared immediately or saved for future audiences of peers, teachers or caregivers.

Storymaking with Popplet

The Popplet app assists children to structure their thinking visually and to develop connections between ideas and concepts. Usually used for mind-mapping with older children in educational settings, Popplet was used in the project to assist the preschool children to develop story structures. The children created stories in a storyboard structure akin to story planning devices used for film and television production that can be defined as a story map. Popplet requires adult support for a preschool child to develop a finished product. From the artefacts gathered during the project it became clear that Popplet can be used to develop both imagined stories and story recounts from real-life experiences. Figure 5.1 overleaf is an example of one child's story about the green sheep. This story is a child's innovation on the text *Where is the Green Sheep?* (2004) by Australian children's author Mem Fox.

While the finished story map looks relatively simple in its construction, there are a number of critical and creative thinking skills at work. The statement on critical and creative thinking contained in *Australian Curriculum: The Arts Foundation to Year 10* (2013) makes a direct reference to the use of technologies that provides the basis for the considered inclusion of iPads in preschool settings: 'In creating artworks, students draw on their curiosity, imagination and thinking skills to pose questions and explore ideas, spaces, materials and technologies' (ACARA, 2013, p. 20).

Figure 5.1 An innovation on the text *Where is the Green Sheep?* Created through images and text developed with a preschool child in an adult-supported activity

Source: popplet.com

Reprinted by permission of Popplet

In the creation of this story map about the possible location of the green sheep, the preschool children engaged in imaginative play to develop a possible scenario in answer to the question, 'Where's the green sheep?' To do this, the child, from whom this sample is taken, moves between concrete, abstract and kinaesthetic thinking. To begin, the child had to place himself into the role of the green sheep through his imagination (abstract thinking). The child then had to take this abstract thinking and represent it through physical objects (concrete thinking). Each moment of this story was documented using the camera on the iPad. This required the child to have an awareness of space in terms of the arrangement of the physical objects and the selected shot type (close-up, mid-range, distance) and body position to be able to manipulate the iPad to capture the shot he required (kinaesthetic). He then had to 'synthesise ideas to communicate a message in a media artwork' (ACARA, 2013, p. 21); this process of synthesis involved selecting the photographs to use, importing the photographs into the Popplet app with the assistance of an adult, sequencing the photographs to tell a linear narrative and then writing the text, again with adult assistance, to complete the story map.

A second example using the Popplet app is what can be classified as a narrative recount. Arguably, the most frequently used from of storymaking engaged in by preschool children is that of the narrative recount. A narrative recount is defined as a telling of a factual or real event. These stories are derived from personal experience and are usually based around 'anecdotes and extended re-tellings of everyday events about family, friends, toys and pets' (Mallan, 1991, p. 26). The stories provide a platform for preschool children to see 'real-life relationships between themselves and other being acted out and resolved' (Mallan, 1991, p. 12). Reuben's 'Juice Shop' story is a first-hand recount using photographic images taken on the iPad and imported into the Popplet app that is supported by written text. Figure 5.2 below depicts how Reuben's story looked when it was complete and ready for sharing.

It should be noted that the resultant storymaking products – *Where is the Green Sheep?* and *The Juice Shop* – both depicting real or imagined events, are not dissimilar to art products seen on preschool walls and in the homes of preschool children. Such products are usually made in a two-step process (which we will call the traditional mode) in which the child paints, draws or

Figure 5.2 A narrative recount created through images and text developed with a preschool child in an adult-supported activity

Source: popplet.com

Reprinted by permission of Popplet

collages an image and once complete an adult, most commonly a preschool teacher or teaching assistant, listens to the child tell the story that accompanies the image and transcribes the oral story into written text directly onto the paper on which the image appears. This simple, two-step process is elaborated upon when using an iPad app. Engagement with an iPad and associated apps such as Popplet (technological mode) support both storymaking and therefore associated literacy outcomes as well as meeting the requirement to include information communication technologies in the preschool curriculum.

Regardless of how the art product is made – in what can be described as traditional mode or through a technological mode – there are creative and storymaking processes that are common to both. First, both traditional and technological modes require some adult collaboration to complete the final art product. Second, both modes privilege child voice and allow the child to have agency over what the story is and how the story is to be represented. And finally, both modes are playful and experimental. There is no one right way to communicate a story. Each story is unique to the individual and therefore the representation of the story will also be an individualised process and product.

Apps as avatars of life experiences for young children

There is a historic false dichotomy set up between the live experience and experience that is mediatised. According to Philip Auslander, a live performance and technology theorist, 'a common assumption is that the live event is "real" and that mediatised events are secondary and somehow artificial reproductions of the real' (Auslander, 1999, p. 3). Auslander stated in an earlier publication on the same topic that:

> The live is an effect of mediating technologies. Prior to the advent of these technologies (e.g. sound recording and motion pictures), there was no such thing as 'live' performance, for that category has meaning only in relation to an opposing possibility'.
>
> (Auslander, 1997)

Since 2006 a theoretical field has emerged that marries the two positions – live and mediatised – together. A third position is described by Freda Chapple and Chiel Kattenbelt as 'intermediality' (2006). Intermediality is 'a meeting point in between the performers, the observers, and the confluence of media' (Chapple and Kattenbelt, 2006, p. 12). Within this intermedial environment, storymaking using the iPad and selected apps can be considered as both a live (through the body engaging language, gestures and voice) and digitised experience (mediated through an app) simultaneously, without one being more hierarchical than the other. As other scholars have suggested: 'When traditional forms of dramatic practice are transformed by technology they take on new qualities and produce hybrid forms that require . . . a new vocabulary to understand them' (Carroll *et al.*, 2006, p. 8). Intermedial storymaking activity could be captured under what Auslander terms 'digital liveness'. Digital liveness, to date, has been associated with the practice of live theatre and performance, but it has relevance to the way in which some apps are used by preschool children and how art products made using the iPad are both made and encountered.

Traditionally, live performance involves the performers and the audience – who are both physically and temporally co-present with one another – and liveness is a condition of that synchronicity of time and space. Likewise, this description could be applied to storymaking events that do not involve the use of mobile digital technologies. The digital however is not bound by these conditions; Auslander first proposed the concept of digital liveness describing it as '. . . the creation of the effect of liveness in our interactions with computers and virtual entities' (Auslander, 2012, p. 7). Digital liveness then is concerned with the way attributes of liveness can enhance and deepen the user experience when online or, in the case of our project, mediated through the engagement with an app. Auslander noted that digital liveness is not caused by intrinsic properties of technology, or the particular construction of an audience. Instead it exists in its relation between 'self and other, a particular way of "being involved with something"' (Auslander 2012, p. 10). The final discussion in this chapter centres around Puppet Pals, which explores the concept of digital liveness with preschool children's iPad interactions.

Storymaking with Puppet Pals

Like Draw and Tell, Puppet Pals produces an interactive product and requires adult support early on as children master the icons and buttons to produce their story. The preschool children's enthusiasm for Puppet Pals was captured in an interview undertaken by one researcher in the project. The researcher asked the children an open question and did not guide their response:

Vignette 2

PC = preschool child
I = Interviewer (QUT Researcher)

I: Have you had lots of fun with the iPads? [Chorus of 'Yeah' from children.] You've been enjoying it? What's been the best thing, what's the thing you've loved most about the iPads?
PC: Playing Puppet Pals.
I: Playing Puppet Pals? And why do you like Puppet Pals?
PC: Because you can create your own person.
I: And that's good isn't it. What else can you do in Puppet Pals?
R1: You can make stories.

This interview data shows that children recognise the agency afforded to them that is built into this app. Cassell and Ryokai (2001) note: '[t]here is, then, a need for today's computer-mediated systems to become "child-driven", where children are in control of the technological objects they interact with' (p. 1). Applying Cassell and Ryokai's premise to the project and its child-made output using Draw and Tell, Popplet and Puppet Pals it can be seen that each of the apps allows children to have control over what they tell, how they chose to tell it and when and where the story is shared.

Puppet Pals is an intermedial app that could be described as using avatars to allow children to represent life experience that is both real and imagined. The word avatar comes from the ancient Sanskrit texts: avat_ra meaning descent. It is mostly translated into English as incarnation, but more accurately as appearance or manifestation (*The Oxford English Dictionary*, 1989). More recently, the term has been adopted by the computer gaming industry to mean an icon or figure representing a particular person in a computer game or internet forum. The avatar is created when a child selects a pre-made character or image to represent themselves and/or others. The liveness of the storymaking event is enhanced when children use the option to take a photographic headshot of

Figure 5.3 Preschool children storymaking using Puppet Pals individually within a social context of activity centre activities

Source: polishedplay.com

Reprinted by permission of Popplet

themselves or others, import it into the app and then place the headshot on the body of a selected animated body thus creating an avatar in the image of themselves. By doing so, the child is both present in real time and in a digital space at the same time and thus digital liveness is present. Puppet Pals utilises recording and playback technologies that are natively available in the app. The app allows preschool children to both visually and orally record their story that can be played back at the moment of creation or saved for replay at a later moment. In applying digital liveness to this activity, preschool children are viscerally present in the moment while representing themselves and others using digital avatars.

The use of the app adheres to one of the themes of practice emerging from the project as outlined in Chapter 2, that in an arts-based context apps that require input from the child and allow the child to make independent choices and decisions develop deep learning. This 'creating from scratch' theme is also echoed in the literature in terms of mediatised experiences that can be applied to storymaking. The resulting product developed by a preschool child using Puppet Pals is not dissimilar to rudimentary animation and therefore has application to media arts as well as drama.

Conclusion

As discussed in Chapter 2, the use of iPads and apps such as those profiled in this chapter should not be considered as replacements for storymaking activities that are currently being undertaken by preschool teachers and preschool students. Rather, iPads and storymaking apps provide an additional platform for preschool children and their teachers to make and share real and imagined events through multimodal literacy forms. Therefore the practices unpacked in this chapter should be viewed as complementary.

The analysis of the literature and the child-made artefacts collected in the project reveal four key ideas for practice that should be considered when using an iPad and selected apps for storymaking events with preschool-aged children. These ideas for practice can be summarised as: making time for questioning and reflection in storymaking activities; engaging with apps that natively include textual elements; privileging apps that allow for multi-sensory engagement and selecting apps that allow children agency. Each of these themes is detailed in the following text.

The importance of questioning and reflection to deepen the storymaking event

Building upon the theme outlined in Chapter 2 that 'quality learning requires intervention and redirection by adults', likewise a storymaking event can be enhanced by reflection between the adult (preschool teacher or caregiver) and the child through open-ended questioning. The making and sharing of a story, either real or imagined, is not a monologue, it is a duologue – a dual carriageway of communication. This dialogical process develops in children 'the ability to listen clearly, accurately and perceptively . . . to respond: offering, questioning and proposing in order to sustain conversation, [and] to turn-take: contributing appropriately without blocking, interrupting, pre-empting or cutting others off' (O'Toole and Stinson, 2013, p. 163).

Inclusion of textual element with a foregrounding of oral communication

Storymaking and storytelling are practices that are based in oral expression. It is important then that the selection of apps for use in this context remain true to the root of the art form. As discussed in the literature related to oracy in this chapter there are enormous lifelong benefits for preschool-aged children when there is deliberate inclusion of oral communication experience. 'Dramatic play [and the related form of storymaking], which is a richly embodied and oral medium, is among the primary ways in which children together explore their world, invent new worlds, try out models of behaviour and communication' (O'Toole and Stinson, 2013, p. 161).

Engagement of multiple sensorial elements in the storymaking event

Young children (and we would argue also adults) encounter the word aesthetically. That is, life events are both experienced and remembered through the senses. 'In my opinion, storytelling for small children, especially in group workshops, requires the use of puppets. Words aren't enough, children need to see' (Miscov, 2014, para. 13). What Miscov is describing in the quote is that storymaking, with and for preschool children, should be sensorial. That is, the sharing of the story should engage all the senses of reception used to make sense of a storymaking event. It should include oral components, aural components, visual components and kinaesthetic components in both the making, sharing and responding phases of the story event.

Selecting apps that allow for child agency

In their research report on the use of technology to allow children to engage in storytelling activities Cassell and Ryokai (2001) noted that:

> While computers are increasingly present in the world of young children, there is a lack of computational systems that support children's voice in everyday storytelling, particularly in the context of fantasy play. . . . In particular as a support for children's fantasy and private worlds, there is a need for technologies that listen to children, reflecting the children's own creations rather than providing adult-produced content.
>
> (p. 1)

When Cassell and Ryokai use the word 'voice' in this text they do not literally mean the child's spoken voice, although Draw and Tell and Puppet Pals do allow for voice recording to occur. What Cassell and Ryokai are referring to is the idea of child agency. The sense of agency in our project is to be found in children's and teachers' negotiations with iPads and apps over power and control. The three apps discussed in this chapter are more child-centred than many and allow children some ability to take charge of content, design of the content and the way in which the content will be transmitted to their chosen audience. As noted early in this chapter, the storymaking activities are not true drama activities but the child-centredness in terms of agency is at the heart of drama practice in preschool settings and beyond.

Bonsignore and her colleagues (2013) believe that 'mobile devices can (and should) be tools for storytelling and creative expression' (p. 2). However, to conclude this chapter, it is important to remember that technology on its own does not constitute the storymaking event. The storymaking event is in the telling and re-telling of a real-life or imagined event and the iPad is a technology with which to negotiate storymaking. The inclusion of mobile digital technologies in the learning experiences of preschool children should be seen part of the network of children's broader conceptual and material experiences, as outlined in Chapters 4 and 8. The use of digital technologies changes children's storymaking and the language we use to describe it.

References

Auslander, P. (1997, April). Ontology vs. history: Making distinctions between the live and the mediatized. In *Proceedings of Digital Conference on Performance and Technology*. Accessed January 14, 2013, from http://webcast.gatech.edu/papers/arch/Auslander.html

—— (1999). *Liveness: Performance in a mediatized culture*. Routledge: London.

—— (2012). Digital liveness: a historico-philosophical perspective. *PAJ: A Journal of Performance and Art*, 34(3), 3–11.

Australian Curriculum, Assessment and Reporting Authority (ACARA) (2013, January). *Australian Curriculum: The arts foundation to year 10*. Accessed January 14, 2014, from www.acara.edu.au/verve/_resources/Australian_Curriculum_The_Arts_2_July_2013.pdf

Bonsignore, E., Quinn, A.J., Druin, A. & Berderson, B.B. (2013). Sharing Stories 'in the wild': a mobile storytelling case study using StoryKit. In *Proceedings of the 2011 Annual Conference Extended Abstracts on Human Factors in Computing Systems*. (May 7, 2011), pp. 917–22. Accessed August 14, 2013, from http://dl.acm.org/citation.cfm?id=2491506

Caldwell, B. & Vaughan, T. (2012). *Transforming Education through the Arts*. London: Routledge.

Carroll, J., Anderson, M. & Cameron, D. (2006). *Real Players? Drama, technology and education*. Stoke-on-Trent: Trentham Books.

Cassell, J. & Ryokai, K. (2001). Making space for voice: Technologies to support children's fantasy and storytelling. *Personal and Ubiquitous Computing*, 5(3), 169–90.

Chapple, F. & Kattenbelt, C. (2006). *Intermediality in Theatre and Performance.* Amsterdam/New York: Rodopi.

Christakis, D.A., Gilderson. J., Richards, J.A., Zimmerman, F.J., Garrison, M.M., Xu, D., Gra, S. & Yapanel, U. (2009). Audible television and decreased adult words, infant vocalisations, and conversational turns. *Archives of Pediatrics and Adolescent Medicine*, 163, 554–8. Accessed June 13, 2014 from http://archpedi.jamanetwork.com/article.aspx?articleid=381618

Deasy, R. (ed.) (2002). *Critical Links: Learning in the arts and student academic and social development.* Washington, DC: Arts Education Partnership.

Dewey, J. (1934). *Art as Experience.* New York: Perigee.

Duck Duck Moose (2013). Draw and Tell. Duck Duck Moose. www.duckduckmoose.com/

Dunn, J. (2003). Linking drama education and dramatic play in the early childhood years. In S. Wright (ed.), *Children, Meaning-Making and the Arts* (pp. 117–33). Australia: Pearson Education.

Ewing, R. (2010). *The Arts and Australian Education: Realising potential.* Camberwell, Victoria: ACER Press.

Fiske, E.B. (1999). *Champions of Change: The impact of the arts on learning.* Washington, DC: The Arts Education Partnership and the President's Committee on the Arts and the Humanities.

Fox, M. (2004). *Where is the Green Sheep?* Australia: Penguin Group.

Heath, S.B. (1982). What no bedtime story means: Narrative skills at home and school. *Language in Society*, 11(12), 49–76.

Hetland, L. & Winner, E. (2001). The Arts and Academic Achievement: What the evidence shows. *Arts Education Policy Review*, 102, 3–6.

Mallan, K. (1991). *Children as Storytellers.* Newtown, NSW, Australia: Primary English Teaching Association.

McLeod, J. (1988). *Drama is Real Pretending: An approach to drama curriculum development.* Melbourne: Ministry of Education (Schools Division).

Miscov, D. (2014, March 26). Once upon a time – capturing and animating very young children's stories. *Early Years.* Accessed May 23, 2014, from http://earlyarts.co.uk/upon-time-capturing-animating-young-childrens-stories/

Notion (2013). Popplet. Notion.

O'Toole, J. (1991). *Oracy, the Forgotten Basic: A provocation.* Brisbane: Ministerial Consultative Council on Curriculum.

—— (2009). Art, creativity and motivation. In C. Sinclair, N. Jeanneret & J. O'Toole (eds), *Education in the Arts: Teaching and learning in the contemporary curriculum* (pp. 3–12). Oxford: Oxford University Press.

O'Toole, J. & Stinson, M. (2013). Drama, Speaking and Listening: the treasure of oracy. In M. Anderson & J. Dunn (eds), *How Drama Activates Learning: Contemporary research and practice.* London: Bloomsbury.

The Oxford English Dictionary (1989). Oxford: Clarendon.

Polished Play (2013). Puppet Pals. Polished Play LLC.

Polkinghorne, D. (1988). *Narrative Knowing and the Human Sciences.* Brisbane, New York: State University of New York Press.

Robinson, K. (2011). *Out of Our Minds: Learning to be creative.* Chichester: Capstone Publishing.

Trousdale, A.M. (1990). Interactive storytelling: Scaffolding children's early narratives. *Language Arts*, 164–73.

Ward, S. (2004). *Baby Talk*. London: Arrow Books.

Wynne-Willson, P. (2014, May 20). Drama vs Storytelling. *Early Years*. Accessed May 23, 2014, from http://earlyarts.co.uk/drama-versus-storytelling-whats-difference-early-years/

Chapter 6

Visual arts learning with iPads

Linda Knight and Karen Dooley

Introduction

In this chapter we look at attitudes and opinions about the arts, how these can link to ideas about authentic learning and how beliefs can be challenged when educators first use iPads in their classrooms (O'Mara & Laidlaw, 2011; Shifflet *et al.*, 2012). The chapter begins by considering common perceptions about art and how these popular beliefs and conditions affect and influence how children's art is defined and valorised. We then discuss how popular beliefs about children's art can impact on the opinions adults have about using iPads to make art. The art produced by children using iPads is then discussed through key observations and reflections, and the chapter concludes with some recommendations when selecting apps for making art.

Attitudes toward the arts

Public relationships with visual arts are often highly emotional and highly subjective (positively and negatively so). Within Western cultures, discussions on 'what is art?' commonly surface in popular discourse, with particular artists or artworks subject to critique and even ridicule if they are seen to subvert the accepted meta-cannon of what makes 'good' art. Public reactions to such works are also commonly contextualised against economic valorisations; assigning a monetary value to the work often ignites further outrage. British artist Tracey Emin's installation piece *My Bed* is a good example of how contemporary art that works outside the meta-cannon is received as an artwork. The piece featured an unmade bed that the artist had slept in surrounded by personal belongings and detritus. In addition, it was shortlisted for the 1999 Turner Prize, worth £20,000; although Emin did not win the prize, the famed art collector Charles Saatchi reportedly paid £150,000 for the piece shortly after. The tabloid and popular press variously derided *My Bed* as 'soiled underwear, contraceptive pills, condoms and – inexplicably – two chained-up suitcases . . . it is the centrepiece of an exhibit which might well win the Turner Prize' (Kitchen, 1999); and 'C**p art, perhaps. Pretentious, self-publicizing art, maybe . . . Tracey Emin's filthy old drawers [underwear] are art. But that doesn't mean you have to stick them on your wall' (Parsons 1999). Mainstream reporting takes on an indignation over the monetary values of non-conventional art and positions itself as reflecting the reaction of the general population, and what conventional or 'normal' opinions the population is perceived to hold about art.

In world cultures, the identification of both historic and contemporary art is also open to critique although the public is more cautious about declaring their opinions because the art can often be tied to complex codings associated with symbol systems, rituals and festivals, histories and traditions, identities and cultures. However, art that seems to subvert or contest these cannons can also suffer from popular critique and rejection. Richard Bell, an Indigenous Australian artist and part of the ProppaNOW collective, highlighted the tensions of making work that sits outside a 'white' ideal of Indigenous art: 'White people say what's good. White people say what's bad. White people buy it. White people sell it' (cited in Jopson, 2003). Bell (2002) suggests that the idea of an Indigenous or Aboriginal Australian art market is a contradiction, as it is not determined or controlled by Indigenous people – thus what is seen as authentic Indigenous art is also out of the control of Indigenous people and artists, which affects the regard for art that does not fit these 'white' expectations.

Modernist thinking about art (in essence the development of criteria to check individual artworks against, in order to judge its credibility) has therefore been hugely influential on current popular engagement and understanding. In addition to scrutinising and judging individual art pieces, modernist approaches have also affected how art as a discipline is learnt about. Publications about art often divide and group the art according to chronologies, schools, geographies, and connect the works to contemporaneous theories and philosophies of thought. As Elkins (2002) suggests, 'The sequence of Western periods is central to many peoples' imagination of art history, whether they live in Europe, America or elsewhere' (p. 21). Many canonical texts such as *The Oxford History of Western Art* (Kemp, 2000), *Mexican Muralists* (Siqueiros, 1993), or *The Asian Collections, Art Gallery of New South Wales* (Art Gallery of New South Wales, 2003) are ordered geographically or chronologically and they contextualise the contents of the chapters within the wider events, beliefs and politics of the day. Organising art to fit the structural norms of a book divides art into particular groupings determined by the art historian. Westernised, pseudo-scientific approaches often work at some distance to the actual experiences and thoughts of the artist. Modernism, then, ensnares art by compartmentalising it and anchoring it to certain concepts and contexts and actively separates the art from its maker. Cataloguing and ordering art not only removes the artist from the picture but also assists 'outsiders' (people who do not identify as artists) to look in through the window, as it were. Artworks are also organised by practice hierarchies between painting, sculpture, drawing, printmaking, ceramics, as well as between art and design, and art and craft (Hickman, 2005, p. 11), affecting not only how artists themselves view process (certain art skills or capacities can be admired more highly than others), but in a populist context the general public or those with little critical knowledge of the arts can, in addition to vilifying artists and their works, mirror this hierarchising and rate particular skills more highly than others. At auctions, for example, although contemporary art fetches increasingly higher prices, paintings continue to dominate the highest prices paid for art (see Kazakina & Reyburn, 2013).

Since the Renaissance, then, populist engagement with the arts has consistently placed certain practices over others and Eurocentric/European art over world art because world art has been judged against neoclassical philosophic thought and anthropologic understandings of Indigenous cultures and peoples, which essentially regarded them as 'primitive' (Elkins, 2010; Golomb, 2002).

Classifying and hierarchising also affects how children's art is regarded, and also what forms it should typically take. Since the early part of the 1900s, psychological and educational theorists used the drawings produced by young children to gain understandings of human cognitive growth and development (Baldwin, 1895; Ballard, 1912; Goodenough, 1926). Determining typical age or developmental growth stages segmented children's art by seeking out particular details of their contents, and the theories presented certain symbols or schema as concrete evidence of growth or development (Piaget & Inhelder, 1969). Interestingly, and in contrast to the study of adult-produced art, which separates the work into periods, schools, styles, cultures etc., studies of children's art has historically attempted to flatten much of this difference out (Alter-Muri & Vazzano, 2014; Kellog, 1969; Malin, 2013). Collections of children's art from across the globe have been examined, for example, to extract evidence of identical schemata for symbols such as people, homes, animals, to gain 'a new appreciation of children's graphic productions as insights into their mental life' (Golomb, 2002, p. 10). These examinations (see also Gentle, 1981) are driven by a fascination with why children make imagery and whether imagery somehow acts as a visual 'tick' to indicate the reaching of a cognitive milestone (Milbrath, 1998; Perner, 1991).

Tendencies to classify and homogenise children's art (Gardner, 1980; Gentle, 1981) are prompted because child art discourses are closely intertwined with education discourses. Adult art, by contrast, is tied to a wider range of discourses and therefore, it is received by audiences in many different ways. The impact these differing views have on the art of children and adults is made obvious when, for example, children are thought of as artists. On the occasions when young children create art that is exhibited and sold they are often positioned as child prodigies and sensationalised in the popular press (Huffpost, 2012; Nicholas, 2014). For many children daycare, kindergarten and school is where they encounter, experience and produce art, so some of the tensions around what is conventionally thought of as children's art is interrelated to conventional thinking about education, its main purpose, and how art fits into that (Schiller & Veale, 1996). Child art, at least in the eyes of the general public, primarily performs education-based tasks, these judgements are affected by popular conceptualisations of the key purposes of education. As Robinson (1982) states: 'to those who see education mainly as a preparation for work, it may seem that the arts are unimportant . . . unless they intend to make a career in them' (p. 9). Seeing education as preparation for an adult, working life is common and thus the role of art can often be seen as fun to experience in childhood, but is not likely to be useful in one's future adult career.

The interrelationships between child art and education (with a focus on early childhood and the art of young children) are now further explored to demonstrate how children's art making can be closely controlled and managed to achieve a recognisable appearance. We propose that these expectations are deeply challenged when the more familiar materials for making art in preschool are changed for using an iPad to make art.

Traditions and conventions of art in early childhood

In addition to the associative analyses given to children's art by philosophers, educationalists and psychologists, the meanings, purposes and optimal conditions for supporting the creation of art are also of interest. Ideas about art production within wider early childhood learning and development theories can contextualise interests, with a focus on the particular needs of the very young. The work of two theorists – Montessori and Malaguzzi – are now discussed, because their theories and models on early childhood art education shifted prior thinking about young children's art and these early theorists continue to hold significant influence over contemporary early childhood education.

Maria Montessori was a trained doctor who was interested in the mental capacities of the young. She left the medical profession and in 1907 opened her first children's centre. The programme in place at the centre was based on the medical research she had done with children who had developmental delays, and was based on a premise that young children can direct a lot of their own learning so should be provided with a wide range of activities that they can choose from depending on their preferences and interests. Although the model suggests a freeform approach to education, Montessori initiated control over content and delivery. Montessori felt that young children's drawings, for example, were an indicator that they were ready to write, so drawing exercises are most useful and purposeful when they are controlled. Small drawings of identifiable things, such as geometrical figures, tracings of insects, colouring in pre-drawn imagery, and holding the pencil in a particular way were all seen to assist the child in learning to write as well as to improve future drawing skills. Montessori disregarded the 'useless, immature, weary efforts' (Montessori, 1967, p. 280) of free drawings, seeing them as requiring 'an explanation on the part of the child who drew them as to what is meant by those incomprehensible essays' (p. 281).

Malaguzzi, who initiated a new model of early childhood education in the Reggio Emilia municipality in Italy, did not separate children's art from their other forms of work, rather he centralised it within the entire education experience (Gandini, 2005). He formalised children's art by setting up the schools around the concept of a studio (atelier) with learning overseen by a professionally trained artist-teacher (atelierista). His constructivist approach encourages children to actively engage in negotiating their learning in ways familiar to them rather than using modes preferred or more familiar to the adult:

> It had to be a place favoring children's logical and creative itineraries, a place for becoming familiar with similarities and differences of verbal and nonverbal languages.
>
> (Gandini, 2005, p. 7)

The children's art produced in the Reggio Emilia schools reflected a constructivist approach because the works were seen to possess 'expression of urgency, desires, reassurance, research, hypotheses, readjustments, constructions, and inventions' (Gandini, 2005, p. 9). Malaguzzi recognised that when children create art they discover, take risks, theorise and explore ideas, and that the art can relate to many different concepts and starting points. His constructivist approach, and his placing of a professional artist-teacher at the core of the school to guide and instruct also implies that Malaguzzi employed what is understood as a socio-constructivist method (Learning and Teaching Scotland, 2006): the children were free to express and explore, but they need the knowledge and guidance of the expert to develop their skills and ideas further.

The approaches of Montessori and Malaguzzi highlight how children's art can be romanticised and perceived to require adult intervention and guidance over symbolic and purposeful decisions children might take when creating. The intentions behind intervention might be honourable but these serve to segment children's art, and attribute meanings to it, which in many cases is not accurate to the purpose and intention the child might hold about it. Children's art can be assumed then, to perform tasks that are unlikely to connect with their original purpose. For example, young children can be interested in working through ideas about science, relationships, fictions or sensations. Children might not see these ideas as linked to creating 'art', which can be driven by a desire to increase artistic process or skill, aesthetic finesse, artistic style or theory, public exhibition etc. A young child's intention might not be to consciously produce 'art', but to regard their work as visual inquiry into their growing understandings and ideas about things.

More recent views and theories show a steady theorisation on the signification and meanings in children's art (Atkinson & Dash, 2005; Eisner, 1976). Specialist discourses fuel how adults learn to understand what they see in children's art making (MacRae, 2013), particularly when children's art is interpreted for evidence of developmental milestones, cognitive perception, giftedness, even experience of trauma or abuse. In short, children's art is rarely neutral but is constantly scanned for meaning. Child art discourses then, serve to situate and ground children's creative work, and to control its processes (MacRae, 2013). Crucially, the interpretations that are attached to children's imagery affect how arts activities are delivered to young children because educators provide materials for making an art product that they have already pictured in their mind (Robinson, 1982).

The analyses of child art provided by early childhood theorists continue to hold influence over contemporary kindergartens and classrooms, and play out in the following art education 'truths': art is vital to the all-round education of the child, to be included as equally as other subjects (some positions argue for art for art's sake, others argue for learning through the arts); art is a solitary activity that is very special and sacrosanct; art uses the imagination and demonstrates creativity; the provision of art requires certain materials and contexts. Although supportive and honourable, these signifying practices and presumptions about why children create art make it less likely that educators will initiate activities that challenge these criteria. As a consequence, more critically-informed recent thinking about arts education may begin to topple art education truths. Sherbine & Boldt (2013) discuss how the work of the new literacies movement recognises that children use many texts including literal, verbal, visual, aural, physical in their daily learning to 'make and express meaning in the world' (p. 77). They credit the new literacies movement, described in Chapters 1 and 7, for helping to shift a view that the written, visual and other semiotic modes are somehow separate, mutually exclusive or developmental (in that a child should move from one to the next mode as it matures), or that the written mode is supreme, or able to be used without other simultaneous use of other modes. Sherbine & Boldt (2013) consider the idea of literacies in multiple modes alongside deleuzeguattarian theories of the assemblage, because for them, not only are multiple literacies used but the child is only part of the event that includes other humans, their surroundings, non-human objects, non-physical components. Children constantly move through these events as part of 'an assemblage that included the other children; the game; the computer equipment, chairs and floor; the classroom and all that was in it' (p. 80). For Sherbine & Boldt (2013), children's art is not easily defined because it occurs 'in the spaces between the children, their drawings, and their play' (p. 86).

Critical examinations of art education also now cast their gaze beyond the classroom space, and consider wider discourses of politics, community, gender, class etc. Pfeiler-Wunder (2013), for example, examines discourses and considers how these impact on 'assumptions about what the children "need"' (p. 146) in terms of the curriculum content developed, and perceptions about their goals and learning expectations. Art here is seen as rich with signs; classroom education is regarded as somehow unaffected from the outside world, and that it is a neutral space, immune from influence. Children's art is regarded here as much more than a pleasant or cute image, it is seen to contain information about 'race, gender . . . class, or socioeconomic standing.' (Pfeiler-Wunder, 2013, p. 147).

iPads and young children's visual arts learning

The complexities, definitions and identifications of what is child art can be disrupted when children use an iPad to create visual work. The iPad is part metal, uniformly sized and weighted, expensive, breakable, flat and has a deliberately non-textural, glass surface: the physicality of the iPad alone seems completely unlike the familiar materials of paper, paint, crayons, pencils and modelling dough that are more commonly used by young children. Because these physical differences and the common discourses about children's art can affect how adults and children regard the art made on an iPad, and whether iPads enrich ways for children to make visual art, introducing iPads into a kindergarten setting can expose some of the uncertainties adults have about introducing digital media to the young.

The healthy growth and development of a child's creativity, imagination and expression are rightfully prioritised in early childhood education and care, so how might introducing young children to iPads initiate good-quality art education in ways that are acceptable and sanctioned by educators, carers and parents? Our iPad study observed how tablet technology is regarded and used by the very young. The physical and digital nature of the tablet offered opportunities to investigate how visual work might be produced that is different to other modes of making art in a kindergarten space.

A number of apps were available for use on the iPads in each of the three participant sites; these initiated different learning experiences and skills. The apps focused on in this chapter are Playschool Art Maker (ABC), Sago Mini Doodlecast (Sago Sago), Brushes (Taptrix), and Draw and Tell (Duck Duck Moose). In addition, the photography function of the iPad is also discussed. Playschool Art Maker is a creative art app based on the licensed characters of *Playschool*, a popular preschool education television programme produced by the ABC and available on free-to-air television. Pre-set background images, including constructed environments, blank colours or photos can be filled with objects and characters. Children can drag and drop selections of these into the backgrounds, enlarge and/or animate them. The app has a function to video record, to capture the building of the image as well as a sound recording. Sago Mini Doodlecast is a drawing app that provides children with blank or ideas pages, or the option to take a photograph and then draw over it. A basic selection of tools and colours are available and, like Playschool Art Maker, drawing and sound is captured, which can be replayed to remind the child how they constructed and narrated their image. Draw and Tell offers a similar package in that it too enables recording and playback options; in addition to basic tool, background and colour options the app also offers stencils, stamps and a colouring-in area, which contains blank templates for children to complete. All these apps feature music and spoken instructions to help users navigate through the functions and options. Brushes is a little different: it is a drawing app that is aimed at all ages and thus has a lot more functionality including layering and opacity options, importing photos, tool size and effect choices, colour and hue selection. Images can be saved as photographs and imported back into the app, or layered with other images. There are no spoken instructions or music so the app is more complex than those aimed at very young children but offers better quality tool options. Lastly, the photography function is a standard feature of the iPads provide; it offers zoom and scaling options as well as switching the direction of the lens. Photographs are automatically saved to the photo album, these can then be exported and used as backgrounds in the apps mentioned above.

Introducing iPad technology into kindergartens and homes helps to learn more about the ways in which the technology affects or impacts on children and their families; the visual data from our project considered what is possible for young children to create when using high-level technology. Qualitative data in the form of digital imagery produced on the iPads, focus group interview data and field notes provide rich information from the view of the children, parents and families, and educators who participated in the project. Particularly powerful are the visual data, comprised of the children's digital art produced during the study, because it presents 'the experiences, opinions and perspectives of children' (Thomson, 2008, p. 3) in modes that are more easily governed by them. Sensitivity and caution when using these images must be applied because in undertaking visual based or visually rich research, researchers must acknowledge the interpretive spaces or 'grey areas' around what might reside in visual works, particularly those produced by children (Thomson, 2008). Children were not interviewed about their visual works beyond providing a brief comment on whether they enjoyed using the iPads.

The imagery produced by children, field observation notes, questionnaire responses and interview transcripts expose some key observations and reflections about children's use of iPads in their visual work and art making. The observations and reflections provide starting points to discuss specific issues relating to quality of learning, using new processes, building aesthetic taste, and how apps shape what is produced. The chapter now addresses those key observations and reflections at length.

Quality learning

The visual art apps selected focused on introducing children to digital/virtual photography, drawing, and painting. Apps that combined photography, drawing and painting with activity such as writing, recording and collating were also available for the children to use. Apps were initially selected via a number of criteria including: recommendations by peers such as other educators;

contextual searches within the App Store; App Store promotion; and the researchers' personal app collections. Final choices were settled on via a process of experimentation by the researchers to examine the quality of the effects and tools; the options available for creating saveable files; and usability: that is, that they could eventually be used independently by young children without them needing reading skills or adult assistance. In addition to functionality, apps were chosen based upon the quality of the learning that could take place and whether app content was aimed appropriately at young children. Judgements about quality were directed by whether the app could potentially offer a highly creative and productive visual art experience for the child over any 'official' claim that they were targeted at young children; consequently children were introduced to – and used – apps that were designed for users of all ages. Importantly, through our searches we often came across apps designed 'for children'; however these often seemed too simplistic and over-deterministic. Examples include apps that provide digital versions of pre-drawn templates that children simply press to flood areas with colour. The colouring-in options on some of the book apps discussed in Chapter 1 are another example. Children's artistic learning is enhanced when they are able to trial ideas, make independent decisions and problem-solve, so the apps we selected offered these experiences.

The educators at each site realised that for quality learning to occur they needed to initially explicitly teach around the use of the iPads and articulate to the children how each app was to be used. Once explicit teaching occurred the children became more comfortable with the iPads and more discerning about their preferences for certain apps, although the educators noticed clearly that children preferred apps that utilised game-based learning even if the app had an art-making focus. The same preference is noted in Chapter 1 in relation to literacy apps. The rapid familiarity children demonstrated encouraged the educators to then relax and allow the children to make independent decisions about what they engaged with and for how long. The educators were confident in stepping back because they saw that children did not actually sit on the iPads all day; they were comfortable in leaving them and playing at other things.

Planning became focused on connectivity and how one iPad activity could creatively link different areas of learning. Art-based apps easily connected different programming foci so the iPads became less an independent object than a part of the suite of educational offerings that connected the children's investigations. For example, as discussed in Chapters 1 and 2, children used the iPad to take photos of baby chicks that they had hatched in the classroom and then embedded these pictures into a template with some captions to make posters. In another example, children took photographs and used those to make eBooks with sound recordings of their voice, which they greatly enjoyed reading and re-reading.

The iPads offered impromptu opportunities for creating art and in ways that extended upon the more conventional product-or-process approaches often used in early childhood. Educators were encouraged to take advantage of spontaneous, arts-rich pedagogical decisions in situ; one site, for example, explored a picture book, made paper drawings based on their interpretations of the story and then photographed them and drew on top of the photographs (Figure 6.1). The excitement or novelty of using the iPads encouraged children and adults to seek out moments of interest in relation to the learning programme in place. As an example, one educator noted: 'we have some zucchinis in the garden and they're not growing particularly well, but there are these little beetles on there . . . so photos and drawings of that'. The iPad also offered forays into new skills: photography became a popular medium to introduce concepts of perspective, distance and portraiture as both children and educators realised that the camera technology on an iPad was much easier to negotiate than trying to understand the complexities of a traditional camera.

Quality learning occurred outside the kindergartens too, as parents gained confidence in interacting with children on certain activities. Parents reported feeling more involved in making art and discussing the art with their children than they did with literacy activities. Sharing the excitement of using technology brought about collaborative learning opportunities as apps were explored and trialled and interacted with, and the preferences children had for doing certain

Figure 6.1 Doggie in the Garden. Digital image
Source: Copyright Duck Duck Moose
Reprinted by permission of Duck Duck Moose

things afforded them more power in those interactions, which offered up more reciprocal and complimentary contributions. As is shown in Chapter 7, prevalent understandings of 'literacy', along with the use of alphabet and phonics apps, precluded this type of experience of the written mode.

Although the iPad prompted the exploration of new skills and enhanced interconnected learning, it did not cause a revolution in the kindergarten. Educators did not change their deep beliefs about learning and pedagogy; rather, the iPad became an additional tool to implement their existing ideas and approaches. Theories of learning and development persisted and the iPads did not sway that: the gradual awareness that the iPad, as a tool, did not actually upscale the child's existing artistic capacities but simply offered a broader range of tools. Children were still making conceptual decisions irrespective of using pencil and paper or digital media.

Exposure to new/unfamiliar processes

Children enjoy making visual work and quickly become very adept at using new materials. Even very young children see how effectively visual work elicits 'aesthetic and emotional responses as well intellectual ones' (Thomson, 2008, p. 11). Children are often positioned as being highly creative beings (Kolbe, 2001; Wright, 2003), able to tap into a 'bottomless' imagination and produce meaningful and unique interpretations of the world around them. Children are imaginative but imagination can be contained if materials are always the same: paper, large brushes, bright coloured chalks, crayons etc. Normative discourses around children's art production connect to the points made earlier about conceptions about what is art, and what is child art. When children enter the kindergarten or preschool space they are faced with materials that become clearly coded as 'art materials'; but what if these were to change, be challenged and expanded upon? Adults might view such changes with scepticism, so the project tested what might happen when children are given completely new materials to use. It is important to see what children can produce when they are exposed to new materials, and what might be produced if the 'materials' are digital. Does the introduction of digital media affect or impact upon the children's use of those familiar art materials?

Despite the fears around young children getting hooked on screen-based technology, or that its presence might render the more familiar art materials obsolete, not all children wanted to create art on the iPad. Even when iPads were freely available for use in the classroom, children often maintained their preference for using paper-based materials and continued to produce paintings, sculptures and drawings. Like any other activity, the iPads were preferred by some children and not others. Children did use the iPads when they were available but even the very young mediated that use effectively. Some children who disliked the messiness of painting and usually avoided it actually preferred and enjoyed creating art on the virtual paper surface of the iPad. For these children, the iPad provided a way in to making art.

Apps that featured digital drawing creation were popular. Being faced with a blank sheet of paper can seem intimidating and often a drawer can default to familiar patterns and symbols to 'fill' the area; although a blank surface was often a starting point in the drawing apps used, the other features embedded in the app helped facilitate ideas and experiments. For example, the sticker options in Draw and Tell were seen positively as a visual reference to help children figure out how to draw particular, unfamiliar things, as the North Side preschool teacher explained in an interview:

> I mean you don't know a turtle is a turtle until you see a turtle . . . if you don't see a picture of it or you don't see a live one or . . . if you've never seen one. So until you get that idea that it's a round shape and it's got all these bits well then how are you even going to draw a turtle if you've got no idea?

The attraction of creating digital drawings also encouraged some children to persist with their drawing and art-making skills. The embedded features not only provided assistance in drawing, but offered perfect material conditions: so the paint didn't run, water didn't spill, pencils were sharp, colours didn't smudge. Certainly, children learn by experiencing these real-life trials and errors so, while these perfect conditions certainly raise some concerns about the value of learning through experimentation and consequence, the children were able to give more attention to the compositions, ideas, and details of their art and their visualising skills.

The educators recognised that the iPad cannot replace the experience of creating plastic arts (i.e. painting, clay, construction, paper-based drawing) but that digital art making offers additional and complementary modes of creative production that collectively provides rich arts experiences to young children. Interestingly, the popularity and particular capabilities of the drawing-based apps prompted the educators to find ways to include more drawing and artistic activity in their programming in ways that extended on plastic arts activities. The educators' willingness to use plastic arts activities more broadly across the curriculum might be more to do with how the plastic arts are often seen as mysterious, personal, private and more related to talent than the 'real' learning of school.

Building aesthetic taste in the young

When children use three-dimensional materials to draw, paint, sculpt and print, they are required to physically interact with those materials. Children can be unfamiliar with the materials or with ways to use them (such as how to use tape to stick boxes together or how to mix paint colours together without them becoming muddy). Additionally, young children are developing gross and fine motor skills, which can impact on how materials are selected, used and manipulated (Rule & Stewart, 2002). Children can therefore work slowly and/or quickly to process their ideas, thinking and experiments. However the child works, art production requires the child to make continuous cognisant decisions about the work to take it to completion. These decisions might be small or large scale but the process of production is dependent upon many personal aesthetic judgements as the artwork evolves (Kinnunen & Einarsdottir, 2013). The aesthetic judgements a young child makes might include how to apply paint so that it effectively stays in one place when paper is pinned at an angle to an easel, how to organise materials so that their cardboard sculpture stands up, or more complex choices such as how to visualise sequence, movement, emotion, size, likeness, and to a standard the child is satisfied with. Children's aesthetic taste then develops through a combination of things including making decisions about their artwork in relation or reference to the other things they see around them; exploring design and conceptual ideas and possibilities; and consolidating their intentions effectively.

Recent interrogations of modernist definitions of aesthetic taste (which attach aesthetics to beauty, skill and emotional appeal) contest the dominant, hegemonic dispositions of aesthetics that have previously directed arts curriculum content as well as championing certain skills and attributes in the art produced by children (Anttila, 2013; Freeland, 2001; Knight, 2013; Warburton, 2003). Modernist visions of aesthetics are essentially white, male and Western and have 'a homogenizing effect where cultural differences may become compromised' (Anttila, 2013, p. 114), that is, the attributes of a high aesthetic championed by one cultural group are not likely to be shared by other cultural groups. Despite these shifts in thinking, in the main conventional thinking and understandings of aesthetic taste continue to shape the types of art that children are exposed to and what they are expected to create irrespective of the child's cultural heritage. The physicality of the iPad challenges these conventions somewhat however because the lack of difference between the tactile, dimensional, or material diversity in the art produced in each of the apps may afford some different value judgements by participants (i.e. the work may still be judged for its appeal but may not be regarded as real art).

The visual work children produced on the iPads was rarely described by parents and educators as 'art' but rather was identified by specific descriptors such as drawing, animation and photography. The hesitation in defining digitally produced visual work as art may be down to its lack of physical dimensionality in the way a painting on a piece of paper or a framed print is physical. Adults seemed to prefer to describe the media of the work rather than considering or foregrounding the intention of the work (such as identifying it as a portrait, still life or landscape). Romanticised conventions about the appropriateness of art materials for children (inexpensive, colourful, disposable, paper, glue, crayons, paints) creates a low-level mistrust of the iPad as being appropriate for children to produce art on because it can only virtually present any of these tools. Adult mistrust surfaced through their opinion that children should stick with more familiar (trusted) tools such as a pencil, paper and paints, especially so if a child was seen as 'good' at art. The virtual materials held in the iPad might somehow fall short aesthetically or take the place of 'real' art making. For example, the South Side preschool teacher said: 'I don't ever want to see that technology take over from what we should be doing kinaesthetically'.

By contrast, the introduction of photography to the South Side preschool caused great excitement. Confidence grew rapidly in using the iPad camera and the staff quickly understood how to foreground aesthetics such as framing, perspective and distance in their teaching of photography. Photographs thus became conceptually purposeful as children were encouraged to pause and consider aspects such as framing and subject matter. The South Side teacher explained:

> Photography is the one thing that we've enjoyed the most. It's made the children look through different eyes at things and I'd like them to be more in control of the documentation of their work.

The photography particularly seemed to enhance the children's grasp of artistic and aesthetic concepts more than any of the other art-based apps used. Figures 6.2 and 6.3 exemplify how young children can understand and explore the concept of distance through choosing distant, middle-distant and close-up

Figure 6.2 Exploring distance and composition. Digital photograph

Figure 6.3 Exploring distance and composition. Digital photograph

compositions. The 4-year-old child who took these images clearly grasped and explored not just differing distances, but how to frame each image to maintain its integrity and interest.

The children's high-level visual acuity came as a surprise to some of the educators, who had not expected to see such consistently high-quality imagery. For instance, the South Side teacher responded: 'So yeah it's had a little wow factor with some of their work'.

More detail about the children's photographic work and how it developed material, conceptual and aesthetic knowledge is presented in Chapters 4 and 8. Additionally, in Chapter 1 we show how photography skills developed in term 2 of the project in one of the centres became prior knowledge for a poster-making activity in term 3. The usual materials with which children's artistic works are often made mean that they are often viewed through the interpretive lens of one learning theory or another; the realist nature of photography can strip much of those interpretations away to expose the aesthetic capability the child possesses in terms of framing and selecting images and details.

Apps as commercial products

As a commercial product the iPad can be conceived of as a virtual warehouse within which sit other, independently commercial products. Discussion on commerciality and commodity are essential therefore because the iPad is not quite as 'innocent' a piece of equipment as a sheet of paper and pencils, or of cardboard and masking tape. The iPad costs a lot of money to buy, and additional costs are incurred through downloading apps and providing network connectivity to optimise its functionality, as well as buying a protective casing for the device when using it with small children. The drawing apps chosen, like other apps available, were free or low-cost. Free apps might seem the best choice initially but can contain 'in-app' purchases, which cumulatively cost more in the long run, so there is an assumption that educators will research the potential cumulative costs prior to downloading the app.

The App Store, as part of the suite of online repositories offered by Apple, follows an egalitarian business framework: anyone is able to register, upload and sell their products through the Apple online stores. App creation and distribution can be highly lucrative financially and offers a powerful incentive to developers to create apps for many different purposes and audiences. Anyone with enough technical knowledge can potentially design and sell an app even if that app claims to be educational or targeted at young children. Unlike textbooks, which go through varying processes of peer review, the professional credibility of education-based app designers and the quality of apps is less easy to regulate so the onus is on the end user to make that decision. While this discussion is rich and important to the context of bringing iPads into early learning, here the focus is on art-based apps and considers how apps might determine what can be created. Apps are variously inventive, however the suite of tools embedded in the app always control what is possible. Of course this can be said as much of a wax crayon as the range of tools contained in an app: the question is how does what is contained in the app design affect how a child makes art, and how might they regard the art that they produce, and is that different to other types of art?

One of the great foresights Apple had was to popularise and unify their graphic organisers. Irrespective of the developer, apps now embed these highly recognisable icons into apps to indicate universal actions such as share, export, delete, save, as outlined in further detail in Chapter 4. Graphic symbols were quickly understood by children and assisted them in learning basic functions common to all apps: 'they really understood the way, like what was going to happen next . . . when they clicked onto insert a photo they knew the process' (interview with North Side preschool teacher). Graphic uniformity enhanced the experience and also quickly built up the children's confidence as they became technologically literate. Generally, children learnt the graphic schema easily and were able to navigate through the apps.

Ease of use often connected to the structural design of the app. The voice-recorded soundtrack also offers guidance in how to select and navigate through the app. Children quickly learnt to use apps that had a simple repetitive design: 'if they're a game-based program once they know how to use it, and that's what they look for' (interview with North Side preschool teacher). Doodlecast and

Draw and Tell do not contain many choices: the art tools available include a brush, pencil or crayon effect, in a reduced basic palette; the paper surfaces also are basic, as is the choice of stickers and picture templates. Art apps designed around game-based play provided the biggest motivation to the children to persist and learn the schema. The preferences that children showed for certain apps over others demonstrated that children are discerning in what an app should contain, and how it should provide the experience. Children were able to vocalise their preferences and also if they felt an app was too difficult to understand or use.

Conclusion

The young children who participated in our study showed great competencies for using arts-based apps. The data from the study showed that iPad and app technology can facilitate children's emergent aesthetic understandings as well as help develop early practical skills in two-dimensional and digital arts. The recording function of many of the art apps also encouraged dialogic skills as children recorded descriptions of their image, created narratives, or dramatised the characters in their pictures. Particularly, children showed great skills and sophistication in photography, grasping the concepts of scale and distance and experimenting with these at kindergarten and independently at home. Collectively their experiments with art making demonstrated rapid awareness of artistic concepts and arts appreciation through replaying recordings, discussing their ways of working with adults and each other, and re-taking or re-drawing imagery until they were happy with the results.

The surprise demonstrated by educators and parents about the quality of the children's work such as the children's grasp of composition, perspective and balance in their photography suggests there remain romantic ideas about the art of young children, as being without any meaning, a scribble, not yet developed, but these conventions may shift over time and as iPads become a more common feature of the kindergarten.

Aside from the views of adults, the children did not seem to differentiate or prefer the art they made with the iPads over the art they made with paints, paper, cardboard, collage and other physical materials. The speed of the technology sometimes seemed to impress them but did not seem to stop them continuing to use many different materials in their creative work. The iPad certainly has significant persuasive power however it is unlikely to replace the traditional art tools many children enjoy making art with.

While it is not the intention of the authors to create a 'top ten' list of best art apps, it is possible to recommend some criteria for choosing apps that can enhance children's learning in and across the arts:

- Choose apps that allow for lots of independent decision-making.
- Apps that feature blank backgrounds are better than those that have pre-drawn images in them.

- Apps that have the option to export children's art in a universal format (e.g. PDF), or that can export directly into the iPad photo album are very useful.
- Being able to export files as email attachments or into cloud storage allows for the art to be printed off, emailed to parents or transferred into word documents for reporting.
- Apps that have a recording facility are really useful to provide an extra dimension to static imagery. Children will enjoy creating verbal narratives about their images, and educators/parents will receive extra information about the child's ideas and intentions.

References

Alter-Muri, S.B. & Vazzano, S. (2014). Gender typicality in children's art development: A cross-cultural study. *The Arts in Psychotherapy*, 41(2), 155–62.

Anttila, E. (2013). Choreographed childhoods: patterns of embodiment in the lives of contemporary children. In F. McArdle & G. Boldt (eds), *Young Children, Pedagogy and the Arts: Ways of seeing* (pp. 106–25). New York: Routledge.

Art Gallery of New South Wales (2003). *The Asian Collections.* Sydney: Art Gallery of New South Wales.

Atkinson, D. & Dash, P. (2005). Art in education, critical and social practice. In D. Atkinson & P. Dash (eds), *Social and Critical Practices in Art Education* (pp. xi–xiii). Stoke-on-Trent: Trentham Books.

Baldwin, J.M. (1895). *Mental Development in the Child and the Race.* New York: Macmillan.

Ballard, P.B. (1912). What London children like to draw. *Journal of Experimental Pedagogy*, 1, 185–97.

Bell, R. (2002). Bell's Theorem: Aboriginal art – it's a white thing! *Koori Web*, November 2002. www.kooriweb.org/foley/great/art/bell.html Accessed 1 February 2014.

Eisner, E.W. (1976). *The Arts, Human Development, and Education.* Richmond, CA: McCutchan Publishing.

Elkins, J. (2002). *Stories of Art.* London: Routledge.

—— (2010). *Visual Cultures.* Bristol: Intellect.

Freeland, C. (2001). *But is it Art? An introduction to art theory.* Oxford: Oxford University Press.

Gandini, L. (ed.) (2005). *In the Spirit of the Studio: Learning from the atelier of Reggio Emilia.* New York: Teachers College Press.

Gardner, H. (1980). *Artful Scribbles: The significance of children's drawings.* New York: Basic Books.

Gentle, K. (1981). The development of children's art, Education 3–13. *International Journal of Primary, Elementary and Early Years Education*, 9(2), 20–4.

Golomb, C. (2002). *Child Art in Context: A cultural and comparative perspective.* Washington, DC: American Psychological Association.

Goodenough, F. (1926). *Measurement of Intelligence by Drawings.* New York: Harcourt, Brace & World.

Hickman, R. (2005). *Why We Make Art and Why It Is Taught.* Bristol: Intellect Books.

Huffpost (2012). 10 Art Prodigies You Should Know (PHOTOS, VIDEOS). 27/7/2012, 624 am. www.huffingtonpost.com/2012/07/27/art-prodigies_n_1699565.html#slide=1271651 Accessed 29 January 2014.

Jopson, D. (2003, November 15). Whitefella Dreaming. *Sydney Morning Herald*. www.smh.com.au/articles/2003/11/14/1069027174339.html Accessed 1 February 2014.

Kazakina, K. & Reyburn, S. (2013, December 24). Bacon $142 Million Tryptich Beats Warhol: Top 2013 Auction Sales. *Bloomberg Washington Newsletter*. www.bloomberg.com/news/2013–12–24/bacon-142-million-triptych-beats-warhol-top-2013-auction-sales.html Accessed 29 January 2014.

Kellogg, R. (1969). *Analyzing Children's Art*. Palo Alto, CA: National Press Books.

Kemp, M. (2000). *The Oxford History of Western Art*. Oxford: Oxford University Press.

Kinnunen, S. & Einarsdottir, J. (2013). Feeling, wondering, sharing and constructing life: Aesthetic experience and life changes in young children's drawing stories. *International Journal of Early Childhood*, 45(3), 359–85. DOI: 10.1007/s13158–013–0085–2

Kitchen, C. (1999, October 20). The dirty bed that could bring Emin a Turner prize. *Daily Mail*: London, 24.

Knight, L. (2013). Not as it seems: Using Deleuzian concepts of the imaginary to rethink children's drawings. *Global Studies of Childhood*, 3(3), 254–64.

Kolbe, U. (2001). *Rapunzel's Supermarket: All about young children and their art*. Byron Bay: Peppinot Press.

Learning and Teaching Scotland (2006). *The Reggio Emilia Approach to Education*. www.educationscotland.gov.uk/earlyyears/images/ReggioAug06_tcm4–393250.pdf Accessed 27 June 2014.

MacRae, C. (2013). Teacher, researcher and artist: Thinking about documentary practices. In F. McArdle & G. Boldt (eds), *Young Children, Pedagogy and the Arts: Ways of seeing* (pp. 50–70). New York: Routledge.

Malin, H. (2013). Making meaningful: Intention in children's art making. *International Journal of Art & Design Education*, 32(1), 6–17.

Milbrath, C. (1998). *Patterns of Artistic Development in Children: Comparative studies of talent*. Cambridge: Cambridge University Press.

Montessori, M. (1967). *The Discovery of the Child*. New York: Random House.

Nicholas, S. (2014, January 22). Show me the Monet: Artist Kieron Williamson earning millions at the age of 11. *Express*. www.express.co.uk/news/uk/455256/Show-me-the-Monet-Artist-Kieron-Williamson-earning-millions-at-the-age-of-11 Accessed 29 January 2014.

O'Mara, J. & Laidlaw, L. (2011). Living in the iworld: Two literacy researchers reflect on the changing texts and literacy practices of childhood. *English Teaching: Practice and Critique*, 10(4), 149–59.

Parsons, T. (1999, October 25). Tony Parsons' column: Turner Prize candidate. *The Mirror*: London, 8.

Perner, J. (1991). *Understanding the Representational Mind*. Cambridge, MA: MIT Press.

Pfeiler-Wunder, A. (2013). Social class and art room curriculum. In F. McArdle & G. Boldt (eds), *Young Children, Pedagogy and the Arts: Ways of seeing* (pp. 146–68). New York: Routledge.

Piaget, J. & Inhelder, B. (1969). *The Psychology of the Child* (trans: Weaver H). New York: Basic Books.

Robinson, K. (1982). *The Arts in Schools: Principles, practice and provision*. London: Calouste Gulbenkian Foundation.

Rule, A.C. & Stewart, R.A. (2002). Effects of practical life materials on kindergarteners' fine motor skills. *Early Childhood Education Journal*, 30(1), 9–13.

Schiller, W. & Veale, W. (1996). The arts: The real business of education. In W. Schiller (ed.), *Issues in Expressive Arts: Curriculum for early childhood* (pp. 5–14). Australia: Gordon & Breach.

Sherbine, K. & Boldt, G. (2013). Becoming intense. In F. McArdle & G. Boldt (eds), *Young children, Pedagogy and the Arts: Ways of seeing* (pp. 73–87). New York: Routledge.

Shifflet, R., Toledo, C. & Mattoon, C. (2012, May). Touch tablet surprises: A preschool teacher's story. *Young Children*, 36–41.

Siqueiros, O.R. (1993). *Mexican Muralists*. London: Lawrence Kind Publishing.

Thomson, P. (ed.) (2008). *Doing Visual Research with Children and Young People*. London: Routledge.

Warburton, N. (2003). *The Art Question*. London: Routledge.

Wright, S. (2003). *The Arts, Young Children, and Learning*. Boston, MA: Pearson Education.

Chapter 7

In and out of preschool learning with iPads

Karen Dooley and Sandra Gattenhof

Introduction

Two visions of home–school relations around the iPad emerged soon after the release of the device. In one, the iPad is used to 'connect' learning in the home with that in school (Northrop & Killeen, 2013) or to enable the home to 'supplement' what is learnt in school (Brown & Harmon, 2013). In this vision, phonics and alphabet apps would be used at home, for example, to practise and reinforce school learning. In the other vision, it is school practices that change as teachers take inspiration from the ways young children use the iPad at home (O'Mara & Laidlaw, 2011). This is a vision of the invention of new practices of schooled literacy education that enable children to be the creative designers and experts in the classroom that they have been observed to be in the home (see also Burnett, 2010). These two visions differ in several ways: in their understandings of the nature of literacy; in their response to the dominance of print-based literacy in formal education; and in their view of the development and acquisition of literacy (e.g. Compton-Lilly *et al.*, 2012; Hassett, 2006). In this chapter we describe and explain the ways we negotiated these same epistemological tensions and structural realities as we implemented the iPad loan component of the project reported in this book (hereafter: 'iPad loan programme').

Children who participated in the iPad loan programme were able to take home one of the project iPads used in their preschool centre, much as they were able to take home books and puzzles. This component was one reflection of the ethos of 'digital inclusion' that infused the project. As we noted in the introduction to this book, there is international recognition of the role that schools can play in ensuring all communities can participate in digital culture and the digital economy (e.g. European Commission, 2014; United States Government, 2013). Accordingly, we conducted the project in preschool centres where at least some groups of children were thought to enjoy less access to learning on digital platforms than others. Our goal was to put the iPad into the hands of children who might not otherwise have had access to it, while supporting teachers and parents in capitalising on the learning potential of the device for all the children. Centres nominated for the project by administrators in the preschool system all served communities that were either affected by poverty and/or diverse in language and culture.

As we came to know the three centres and some of the families, we found a range of technological access and tablet use. One centre already had four iPads, although these had been bought for use with special needs children the year before the project and had not been incorporated into the regular preschool programme.

Home access to tablet technology varied also. A survey administered to the 29 parents who elected to take part in the iPad loan programme found that 5 used tablets with their children 'every day', 10 'several times a week', 3 on 'special occasions', and 11 'never'. With respect to learning activities, 14 of the parents said they used tablets for 'literacy' (understood narrowly as letter and sound recognition) and 11 said they used it for 'storytelling', an activity that can be encompassed within a broader understanding of 'literacy'. With respect to other mobile technology, 7 parents used smartphones with their children 'every day', 8 'several times a week', 9 on 'special occasions and 5 'never'. With respect to smartphones, 14 parents said they used them for 'literacy' and 7 for 'storytelling'. Parent expertise with iPads also varied considerably. A few parents had extensive experience of the iPad and other digital technologies in their

Table 7.1 Selected results from parent survey

Do you currently use any of the following digital devices to develop or implement learning experiences?

	Every day	*Several times a week*	*On special occasions*	*Never*
Smartphones	7	8	9	5
Tablets	5	10	3	11

What types of learning activities do you use the digital devices for?

	Literacy	*Numeracy*	*Visual art*	*Story telling*	*Music*
	Letter and sound recognition; text orientation	*Counting, grouping, spatial awareness*	*Colour and shape; patterns*	*Self ; directed oral; listening*	*Rhythm, sounds, singing*
Smartphone	14	13	16	7	17
Tablet	14	12	14	11	14

professional and home lives; others had considerably less experience although smartphone experience was common. For some of the adults then, the project provided learning opportunities relating to the operation and educational use of the iPad. From our data it is not possible to ascertain how representative these parents were of the parent groups in the three centres.

We look here at the iPad loan programme as a 'family literacy' initiative. By 'family literacy' is meant the literacy-related beliefs and practices of families (Compton-Lilly *et al.*, 2012). When it was first coined by Denny Taylor, the term construed literacy as intrinsic to the social processes of the everyday life of families. It has since been extended to denote the ways that literacy is used and learnt as part of everyday life in home and community. The issues of justice and diversity with which we grappled in the iPad loan programme are common in family literacy programmes and the object of considerable scholarship. Within the structural realities of education systems that privilege certain print-based literacies (Hassett, 2006), these issues articulate with and are played out in competing epistemological stances on the nature of literacy, the goals and purposes of literacy, and the development and acquisition of literacy (Compton-Lilly *et al.*, 2012).

In this chapter we describe and explain some of the epistemological commitments of the iPad loan programme and its participants. In doing so, we take account of the complex structural realities that will be familiar to scholars and practitioners in other early years settings. These include a national back-to-basics accountability regimen in print-based literacies on the one hand, and the demand for what we described in the introduction to this book as the 'digital basics' on the other. Our aim in this chapter is to explore some ways of thinking about iPad-based family literacy programmes in such contexts.

We develop the chapter in four sections. First, we look at how practitioners and scholars have approached family literacy, highlighting some of the tensions relevant to our work here; second and third, we use an epistemological approach recently developed in the field of family literacy scholarship to describe and explain the iPad loan programme and what we learnt from the programme. Fourth, we conclude by returning to the visions of home–school relations around the iPad.

Approaching family literacy

Issues of justice and diversity are integral to many family literacy initiatives – and the object of considerable contention. For more than 30 years, family literacy programmes have been viewed as a cure for poverty and social ills. Most recently, this has seen them framed in neoliberal and neoconservative discourse, prompting concern that they are being used to shift responsibility for addressing social and economic inequality from the public sector to exploited and marginalised individuals and families. Further, the programmes have been criticised for their colonising work in imposing the storybook literacies and school-like tasks valorised in middle-class homes on minority families and families affected by poverty (Compton-Lilly *et al.*, 2012).

To elaborate, the 'story literacy' we described in Chapter 1 has long been implicated in social reform agendas. At the beginning of the twentieth century, literature along with the arts and nature were all enlisted by the kindergarten movement to 'save' underprivileged children from the influences of their homes (Marsh, 2003). At the century's end, literature was entrenched even more deeply in early years education as the concept of emergent literacy valorised the storybook reading and writing practices of middle-class homes. Indeed, storybook reading became the favoured vehicle of reading education. Shared book reading, for example, was developed in the 1960s as the New Zealand capital, Auckland, 'became a fully-fledged modern city with a new type of inner-city school . . . characterised by poverty and a rapid influx of migrant people' (Holdaway, 1979, p. 7). The approach was an attempt to create for all children in school the conditions that enabled some children in privileged homes to learn to read 'naturally'. Storybook reading was at the core of the approach:

> [b]ecoming literate is greatly facilitated by a natural familiarity with and love of book language—ideally the learner identifies himself [sic] with the dialect of books and lays personal claim to it.
>
> (Holdaway, 1979, p. 17)

The dominance of storybook reading and writing in literacy education is one instance of a social dynamic by which literacy instruction and subject English transmit 'forms of communicative practice that are . . . understood to be somehow different from other forms of communicative practice' (Heller, 2008, p. 54). 'Different' here implies 'superior'. Historical accounts show that with the rise of the capitalist nation-state, the communicative practices designated as 'literate' were construed as ways of thinking suited to the pursuit of social order and progress and distinguished thereby from everyday language practices. This represents what Brian Street (1984, 1997) referred to as an 'autonomous' model of literacy. By this model, literacy is a universal cognitive skill implicated in the development of logic, rationality, empathy and other supposed benefits.

Cultural mismatch hypotheses have been used widely to explain the inequitable distribution of storybook literacy. The original account of shared book reading pointed to 'alienation' from and 'fear' of the bookish dialect of school learning. And it prescribed immersion in that language as the means of redress: 'A fine literature can form the bridge across cultural difference to literate language' (Holdaway, 1979, p. 17). The assumption was that children would be drawn into literate language by 'literature at its best', by books that transcended what were thought of as 'surface distinctions of cultural difference' to address 'universal human concerns' (Holdaway, 1979, p. 17). Critics went on to argue that there was more to the problem than linguistic content alone, pointing to the form of teacher–student interactions around books as a source of difficulty (Luke, 1992). This is a criticism inspired by the anthropological work of Shirley Brice Heath (1982).

Unlike Holdaway (1979), Heath was concerned not with the cultural content of books – 'fine' literature or otherwise – but with the socio-cultural specificity of the activity of literacy itself. Her work in the south-eastern United States showed that what counts as literacy is culturally located and socially contingent. It documented the different 'ways of taking' from books prevalent in three literate communities: a town community with a mainstream, middle-class culture oriented to school; a white, working-class community of Appalachian origin; and a black, working-class community of rural origin. It was the children from the first of these communities who found school most familiar. From their home socialisation experiences, the middle-class children valued books and acknowledged their authority as was required in school; moreover, they were accustomed to the interactive routines around books enacted in school. It was concluded that 'the mainstream type of literacy orientation is not the only type even among Western societies'; moreover, 'mainstream ways of acquiring communicative competence do not offer a universally applicable model of development' (Heath, 1982, p. 73).

In the spirit of Heath's (1982) own theoretical perspective, some researchers (Hill & Nicholls, 2009) have noted that her findings relate to particular socio-cultural contexts. They cite Australian research that showed the pedagogies of some working-class families meshed with those of the school in ways that the pedagogies of some professional families did not. Specifically, the working-class families in question enacted school-like pedagogies at home, thereby socialising their children into the type of interactions they experienced in school; in contrast, the professional families granted their children greater rights of participation than their teachers did, thereby rendering school a somewhat uncomfortable place for them. The point is that Heath's theoretical principles are broadly applicable, but characterisations of middle- and working-class communities in places, times and institutional contexts other than those she investigated cannot simply be read off her empirical findings.

In the 30 years since Heath's watershed study, many researchers have gone on to document the diversity of everyday out-of-school literacies, especially in minority communities and communities affected by poverty (e.g. Purcell-Gates, 2007; Taylor, 1983). More recently, this type of research has been extended to literacy practices on digital platforms (e.g. Larson & Marsh, 2005; Pahl & Rowsell, 2005). Together, these studies paint a picture of a diversity of literate worlds rich in the multilingual, multicultural and multimodal practices of everyday home and community life.

Interestingly, some studies of literate practices on digital platforms point to mismatch between literate ways of being and doing acquired by privileged middle-class children in the home and those valorised in school (e.g. O'Mara & Laidlaw, 2011). They show children growing up with dispositions to digital-based texts as multimodal and spatially organised artefacts that are re-designable by the user. But these children enter schools where it is the disposition to treat text as monomodal and linear artefacts composed by an author for interpretation by readers that is valorised. In this situation there is talk of 'English curriculum . . . coming unstuck' because of a 'clash of worldviews, dispositions and what is valued in school' (O'Mara & Laidlaw, 2011, p. 157). By this account, the burden for change rests on teachers and the school.

Ethnographic understandings of family literacy might have catalysed changes in the literacy education practices of the school, but generally that has not been the case. Instead, it has been the practices of the family that have been targeted for change through family literacy programmes. This has been especially true for children affected by poverty and/or living in linguistically and culturally diverse communities. As a result, there has been 'growing curricularisation of out-of-school literacy practices' of minority and poverty-affected communities; school practices have not been penetrated by the practices of the homes within those communities (Marsh, 2003, p. 370).

The engineering metaphor at the heart of the shared book-reading approach – the need for a bridge between cultures – is found in the family literacy literature, too. There is much talk of the need for 'bridges' and 'pathways' between home and school; and further, of the necessity for two-way traffic across and along these, as distinct from the one-way flows from school to home that have typified home–school relations (e.g. Hill & Nichols, 2009; Marsh, 2003; Williams-Kennedy, 2009). Others invoke a geographical metaphor, speaking of home, community and school as literate 'worlds', and children, as border-crossers (Hill & Nichols, 2009).

The 'worlds' metaphor is employed in a study of 4-year-olds in a multilingual English nursery school (Kenner, 2000, p. 87). In this study, texts from the literate worlds of minority homes and a linguistically and culturally diverse community were brought into the classroom to make the literate world of the school a more familiar place for the children. These texts were described as 'home pages'. Parents, children and teachers went on to create new home pages by working together in the nursery to build on understandings of literacy acquired in family settings. Ten years before the release of the iPad, it was imagined that the 'home pages' of the 'future' would be electronic and multimodal – literally, the home pages of the web. Young children, it was supposed, would be able to represent themselves in image and writing on these home pages while engaging in dialogue with the audiences of cyberspace. The aim was a two-way traffic of text, representation and practice among a child's literate worlds (Kenner, 2000, p. 88) in order to create literacies that are neither of home nor school but of both worlds simultaneously.

A major review of family literacy scholarship recently made the case for going beyond the binaries of the field: home/school and match/mismatch included (Compton-Lilly *et al.*, 2012). These binaries assume that the literacies in children's lives are separate, an assumption that belies evidence of synergism and hybridity, of the way children mesh the stuff of the literacies of the media with that of those of the home or school, for example. Moreover, the binaries do not account adequately for strategic action, for instance, the pursuit of schooled literacies in minority communities in contexts of high-stakes testing. In seeking an alternative approach, Compton-Lilly and colleagues (2012) note the interplay of modernist and postmodernist epistemological considerations in the work of diversity scholars in general and diversity-oriented family literacy scholars in particular. They attribute this apparent contradiction to tension between aspirations for success in established school practices and for cultural self-determination through transformation of those practices. They go on to suggest an epistemological approach to analysis of family literacy initiatives that enables account of this complexity. This entails attention to assumptions about: (1) the nature of literacy; (2) the goals and purposes of literacy; and (3) the development and acquisition of literacy.

We, too, grappled with these three epistemological issues in designing and conducting the iPad project – and continue to do so through the various theoretical lenses the writing pairs have brought to the chapters of this book. In the next two sections of this chapter, we use the epistemological approach to help us describe and explain the iPad loan programme; then we use it to look at some of the things we learnt from the programme.

The iPad loan programme

The iPad loan programme began after the iPads had been used for about a term in the preschools and continued until the end of the preschool year and the project three terms later. Families began taking the iPads home on loan after a start-up workshop presented by teachers and teacher-aides in each centre and one or two researchers. The workshops and iPad loan programme were organised slightly differently in each preschool; here we look closely at those that occurred at Southern Preschool. We feature this centre not because it was indicative or exemplary, but because it enables some reflection on iPad-based family literacy programmes for diverse communities. Furthermore, one of us was the researcher attached to this centre and so brings participant-observer data and interpretive background to the chapter.

As we noted in the introduction to this book, Southern Preschool serves a linguistically and culturally diverse community 15km from the Brisbane CBD. In the surrounding suburbs there are significant concentrations of immigrants from Taiwan, China, Vietnam and India and a majority group population that includes a mix of working-class and professional families. In what follows, we draw on several sources of data about the iPad loan programme at this centre: participant-observer notes from the start-up workshop; documents produced by the teacher and researcher for use in the workshop; and two rounds of interviews with parents, children, teachers and teacher-aides conducted one and five months after the workshop, and in the case of the teacher, another interview conducted at the end of the project, seven months after the workshop.

Table 7.2 Parent iPad Workshop, April, 2013

7:00 pm	5 min	Welcome and introductions
7:05 pm	10 min	How to use iPads
7:15 pm	5 min	Overview of the project
7:20 pm	30 min	Creativity with iPads [teacher] – sharing student work with Brushes
7:50 pm	30 min	Storytime with the iPads [researcher] *The Cat in the Hat Comes Back* *Close my Eyes* *PopOut Peter*
8:20 pm	10 min	Home use of the iPads
8:30 pm		Survey and refreshments

The start-up workshop at Southern Preschool was attended by 19 parents – approximately three times as many the number of participants at each of the other two centres. From our data set it is not possible to ascertain the reason for this disparity of participation among the centres. The agenda for the workshop we conducted with the 19 parents is presented in Table 7.2. We now look briefly at the content covered by several items on the agenda, namely those relating to operational skills and educative uses of the iPad.

Operational skills for iPad technology

In this segment of the workshop parents were given the project iPads to handle. For those who were unfamiliar with the device, the teacher spent a few minutes demonstrating how to turn the iPads on and off, operate the screen by touch, select an app, and use the home button. Participants were then able to try these operational moves out for themselves. Technical terminology was used to name parts of the technology (e.g. 'home button') and parents were encouraged to use this terminology with their children. As the following excerpt from a PowerPoint slide used in the workshop shows, an analogy was drawn with the use of the terminology for describing the technology of the print book. On reflection, it is apparent that the researcher made an assumption here about the way parents interacted with children around books; parents were assumed to talk like a teacher conducting shared book reading sessions:

Teaching tip: Use the technical language with children (as you use words like 'cover', 'title', 'author', 'spine', 'page', 'line', 'word', 'letter' and so forth when talking about books).

For some of the 19 participants, this was the first time they had operated an iPad; for others, it was an opportunity to share some of the 'tips' and 'tricks' they had picked up from their own sometimes extensive iPad use. For example, one woman noted that we had omitted to look at how to close apps. When we said that we did not know how to do that, she demonstrated the procedure, drawing an analogy to the difference between closing and minimising a program on a computer.

A transmissive but collaborative pedagogy was in place during this part of the workshop: 'experts' demonstrated for others to copy. This was the same pedagogy employed in the classroom to teach the children skills for operating the device (see Chapters 1 and 3). An epistemological position seems to be emerging in this regard: like pencil use and book handling, perhaps, the operational skills for the iPad use are efficiently transmitted through direct instruction. Only, at the present time, the person with the expertise required of the transmitter of basic digital operational skills is not necessarily the person with the content expertise.

Educative uses of the iPad

This component of the workshop was conducted by both the teacher and the researcher. The teacher spoke on the use of creating apps while the researcher spoke on the use of iBooks.

The teacher showed the parents some of the products that had resulted from the children's exploration of the creating app, Brushes. She used the Mondopad – a touch-screen tablet large enough to be read across a classroom – to project an iBook she had created from the children's drawings. While doing so, she pointed out what the children had learnt, explained why she was satisfied with the quality of that learning, described the facilitative pedagogy she had employed, and encouraged parents to continue this work with their children during the iPad loan scheme. She also told the parents about the photography learning experiences she was currently providing the children in the centre.

The researcher used the Mondopad to project a 5-slide PowerPoint presentation on 'Storytime with the iPads'. She opened her presentation by making the point that iBooks can be used to create rich adult-child story reading experiences. The epistemological position here is that literacy learning can be mediated by adults through talk (see Chapter 3). This socio-cultural understanding of the development and acquisition of learning is consistent with that found in emerging research on iPad-embedded storybook reading (e.g. Morgan, 2013; Neumann & Neumann, 2013; Roskos *et al.*, 2012) and a somewhat more established body of research on online storybook reading (e.g. Fisch *et al.*, 2002).

The researcher also made the point that literacy is a multimodal process, illustrating this with a diagram informed by the New London Group (1996) model of 'the what' of multiliteracies instruction. In this model, the linguistic, visual, audio, spatial and gestural modes all count as 'literate', as do multimodal configurations of these (see Chapter 1). This epistemological position on the nature of literacy is consistent with national and state level policy in the early years sector. At the national level, the Early Years Learning Framework (EYLF) understands literacy as:

> the capacity, confidence and disposition to use language in all its forms . . . [It] incorporates a range of modes of communication including music, movement, dance, storytelling, visual arts, media and drama, as well as talking, listening, viewing, reading and writing. Contemporary texts include electronic and print-based media.
>
> (Australian Government, 2009, p. 38)

Consistent with the EYLF, 'communication' is an organiser in preschool-level curriculum in the state in which the study was conducted. According to this policy, the child is to become an 'effective communicator' who 'explores and engages with literacy in personally meaningful ways'. Significant literacy learnings include 'positive engagement with a variety of print and multimedia texts and the arts' (The State of Queensland, 2010, p. 61).

Finally, the researcher took an epistemological position on the goals of literacy. She described the potential of iPad-embedded storytime for achieving 'the basics' such as comprehension that are assessed by national literacy tests, and the 'digital basics' for twenty-first century educational participation, for instance, multimodal reading processes. This is a position found in the professional literature (Hutchison *et al.* 2012). According to the continuum of interactivity (Rowsell, 2014) we used in Chapter 1, comprehension is an appropriate goal for multimodal iBooks given the linearity of these texts and the control the narrative exercises over the reader. In preparing for the workshop, the researcher explicitly adopted this overtly school-oriented epistemological position because of knowledge – gleaned from several research projects in the suburb over a period of more than 20 years – of the literacy practices and expectations of at least some groups in the local community.

Together, the teacher and the researcher sought to influence family use of the iPad. As we put it in our application for funding, the intent was to 'demonstrate how [parents] . . . can use iPads to read to their children and assist their children to use iPads to communicate their ideas in playful and productive ways'. In doing this, we promoted home literacy practices that would mesh with the preschool practices we were developing with the teachers for the use of a relatively new digital platform.

While the iPad loan programme was clearly modernist in its promotion of school-sanctioned literacies, there was a dialogic element to it. As is evident from the visions of home–school relations around the iPad with which we opened this chapter, a discourse urging schools to seek inspiration in the playful, creative, multimodal literacy activities of the home is currently in circulation in literacy education forums. But given awareness of more than three decades of family literacy scholarship, the researcher was wary of the risk of imposing on families practices abstracted from the practices of families in other socio-cultural contexts. The research component of the iPad loan programme was designed to open up dialogue with families around their iPad-embedded literacy practices. Accordingly, the teacher and researcher emphasised that their ideas for home use of the iPads were precisely that: their ideas. Parents were encouraged to use the iPads as they wished with their children and then to let us know what they had done. We made it clear that we were seeking to learn from them about how they used the iPad at home and that our goal in doing so was to inform preschool practice and future preschool–home relationships around the iPad. In this way we tried to build some dialogue into the research relationship. We turn now to some of the learnings that resulted.

What we learnt from the iPad loan programme

Here we present three of our learnings from the iPad loan programme. These relate to (1) the failure to recruit a representative number of minority group families as programme participants; and (2) the educative uses of the iPad in the home favoured by participating families. We now look at each of these learnings in turn.

Participation in the programme

Although Southern Preschool has a linguistically and culturally diverse population, the iPad loan programme at the centre did not. Of the 19 families from the centre who participated in the programme, only three were from minority groups. This was disappointing because the centre had been selected for the project on the grounds of its diverse clientele; we had not anticipated this pattern of participation. The teacher suggested that the participation pattern might have reflected differences of experiences in term 1. Most of the minority children were in the one class. The teacher said that negotiating the language barrier in order to settle that class into preschool routines had been time-consuming; she had not had the time to introduce the iPad in the way she had been able to in the other class.

From the data it is not possible to verify the teacher's explanation. But it is cause for consideration because the teachers in one of the centres serving a community affected by poverty attributed their relatively slow start to the project to the time it took to settle a constant stream of new enrollees into the centre in term 1. There is an epistemological position here that has been noted in some of the other chapters in this book (e.g. Chapters 1 and 3): development and acquisition of iPad literacy requires intensive adult input at the outset. This is a position that may be consequential for children's access to iPad-embedded literacy education in conditions of poverty and diversity.

The uses families made of the iPads

The project iPads were loaded with iBooks (e.g. *PopOut Peter*), and creating apps (e.g. Doodle Buddy), and educational apps (e.g. Reading Eggs). Some of these apps had already been used, to some extent, at preschool before the iPad loan project started. So too had the camera. Families were encouraged to add to the apps on the devices. A letter to the parents at Southern Preschool stated:

> You are free to download any age appropriate Apps or Books to the iPad for use with your child via the App Store or iBooks. However, we recommend that you *do not download any paid Apps or Books* as there will be no way for you to keep them once the iPad is returned to the Kindy [preschool]. Furthermore, you will need an Apple Account to be able to download these materials [original emphases].

We now look at what we learnt about home use of each of these three types of apps. We present data produced with several different families, including those of Sam and Jenny. Sam is a fluent English-speaking boy; Jenny is a Cantonese-speaking girl who primarily uses English at preschool, although she learns English with her mother at home. We feature the data produced with Jenny in order to make some account of the diversity in the preschool community.

Previous research in the same suburb (Chiang, 2010) showed considerable difference between the home literacy experience of 4-year-olds in Taiwanese families and that typically endorsed by majority group teachers, although there were some differences among the Taiwanese families. Those findings are consistent with a proliferating international literature on Chinese family literacy in Western societies (Mu & Dooley, 2014). The data relating to Jenny can in no way be considered representative of minority families in the study or even Chinese families, but they are useful, however, for highlighting the complexity of the terrain on which family literacy programmes might seek to both build on local literacy practices and prepare children from diverse communities for success within the realities of existing educational structures (Compton-Lilly *et al.*, 2012).

Book apps

In Chapter 1, we presented data excerpted from an email interview with Sam's mother. In those data, this parent noted that her son was using iBooks at home. To reiterate:

> He has also just started to read the iBooks on the Kindy [preschool] iPad and his favourite is *Goldilocks and the Three Bears.* He can read the story along with the narrator now and is starting to recognise some small words.

Book apps clearly engage Sam. There were children like Sam in all the centres and their parents spoke of them 'loving' the book apps. One mother spoke also of her interaction with her child being enriched when the book was delivered by iPad. These were the type of experiences the project had been set up to promote. But they were not as common as the researcher had anticipated. iBook use, we showed in Chapter 1, got off to a slow start in the classroom; home use was also somewhat less enthusiastic than anticipated.

Two parents indicated that they made limited use of book apps because they were heeding the teacher's warning about the need to limit screen time to 20 minutes per day. In these conditions, the parents thought book apps were too time-consuming. Jenny's mother was one of these parents. She said that:

> because you are playing, like do 20 minutes, per night, so there's a limit of time you can do because maybe not good for their eyes, yeah, so, but the [print] books you can read for an hour, yeah, there's no time limit.

One parent said that she did not have many book apps on her own iPad and that her child was not keen on the book apps on the preschool iPad. The researcher's response to her statement indicates that this was emerging as a theme of the interviews she was conducting that day.

R: Storybook apps, what's your experience of them vis-à-vis traditional books?
P: I haven't got a lot of storybook ones [on my iPad]. The Kindy one [iPad], she like, I think there's a *Spot* book and all she did was the puzzle. She didn't even, yeah, but
R: You're about the tenth mum who has told me that.

During two interviews earlier that morning, one of the 'ten mums' had said that her child liked everything but the book apps. After listing the educational apps, music apps and drawing apps her son loved, she stated that he was:

> not really interested in the books. Most of them [books], they [my children] go, 'yeah', about half way, and he goes, 'I'm sick of this, can we move on?' Particularly the Doctor Seuss one, he's just not interested and yet he'll let me read a book.

The contrast between this child's interest in print book reading and iBook reading was not unique in the data set. Other parents noted that their children were more engaged by traditional print book readings than by readings involving the iPad. They attributed this to the pleasure of hearing a loved adult's voice read the story. This is a similar position to that taken by the centre teacher. In Chapter 1 we noted that this teacher said the print book had 'precedence' over the iBook in her classroom. She went on to say:

> I guess you, you can't replace a person, and let's hope we don't replace a person, in reading to a child. It's nice to be able to read in your voice, in mum and dad's voice and in the intonation that you can put into a story and that physical touch where they're sitting on you and you've got the

> book here. With the iPad it's not the same, and even with my own granddaughter, with the iPad, it's a little bit less personal with my own granddaughter. 'Sit here', and we sit and look; it's not the same. I don't, I don't get a feel that it's the same that I do when it's a book. There's just a warmer, I don't know.

One of the mothers said her family got around the problem of 'familiar voices' by audio recording stories. Her children loved to listen to the recordings she and her husband had made on the iPad of themselves reading storybooks. For one family, however, the unfamiliar voice was the best feature of book apps. In response to a direct question about whether her daughter used the iPad for Chinese learning, Jenny's mother indicated that she did, naming an app recommended by the teacher at Southern Preschool. She then went on to speak of the use of book apps for learning English:

> it's very good because you can hear their pronunciation and they [the app] will read to you and they [the children] just follow.

In her research in the suburb a few years before the release of the iPad, Chiang (2010) described a parent using an electronic dictionary to get correct pronunciation for their preschool-aged child. The iBook would seem to be a more convenient technology serving this purpose. In one of her interviews, the teacher at Southern Preschool said that iBook reading was producing this same benefit for the many learners of English as an additional language in her centre.

In summary, there is a richness of epistemological position in the parents' talk about their home use of book apps. Much of this is to do with the development and learning of literacy. Parents spoke of children learning by reading along with and talking around iBooks and grappled with learning by listening to familiar and unfamiliar voices. Implicitly, the goal of this learning seems to be reading. But the data produced with Jenny's mother show that this was not the only epistemological position. In Jenny's family good English pronunciation was a goal of iBook reading and listening to an unfamiliar but fluent reader was a means of literacy development and learning.

Creating apps

Sam loved his creating apps as much as his book apps. In her second interview, which was conducted by email five months into the iPad loan programme, his mother reported:

> Sam has continued on his favourite programs (Draw and Tell, Little Fox Studio) that allows him to create works of art and music. He loves to show his dad and brother his creations.

Jenny, too, loved her creating apps – and not just on the iPad:

> drawing, she likes to draw, as well on my phone.

This enthusiasm for creating apps was shared by many of the children. Parent after parent mentioned photography. Children practised the photographic techniques they had learnt at preschool, passed those techniques on to other family members and transferred them to the family iPad or their (grand)parents' smartphones. One parent said that her child did want to practise his photography at home. The reason for this, however, was that he preferred to make movies on his own (brand unspecified, non-iPad) tablet. Another said that her child had already developed good photography skills using the HP Elite tablet she had brought him and his brother prior to the preschool year. In particular, her son enjoyed distorting the images he had captured. While photography was by far the most common creating activity spoken of by the parents, creating music and making up songs were also mentioned.

The children's interview data are similar to the parent data. When asked what they liked doing on the iPad, most of the children mentioned photography. When asked how they had learnt, some said they had learnt at home and others at preschool. One child mentioned the photography 'homework' they were given at Southern Preschool, describing what he had been asked to do at home with the iPad. Drawing apps were also mentioned positively by several of the children.

Given the enthusiasm around creating apps, the researcher was somewhat surprised to be asked by several parents for more educational apps. This request was a response to a question in the first interview designed to elicit suggestions for the next phase of the iPad loan programme.

Educational apps

From our description of the start-up workshop for the iPad loan programme at Southern Preschool, it will be apparent that, although educational apps were available on the iPads, we only mentioned them in passing. For the researcher, this reflected awareness of the goals of the programme – to support parents in iBook reading and playful, productive uses of the iPad – rather than epistemological positions on basic print skills instruction per se. As a lecturer in English curriculum she promotes the use of book apps for basic literacy skills instruction with her own teacher education students.

Our passing references to them notwithstanding, the educational apps received extensive use in the children's homes. Parent after parent, and child after child mentioned them in interview; indeed, when asked to show the researcher what they liked doing on the iPad, some of the children opened an educational app. This is perhaps not very surprising: as we indicated earlier, at the outset of the programme 14 parents had indicated that they used basic literacy skills apps with their children on their iPad and 14 said the same about their use of smartphones. In what follows, there is an account of Sam's experience of educational apps on the preschool iPad; once again, the data have been excerpted from his mother's email interview:

> The other favourite app is the Alpha Tots. He knows almost the entire alphabet now (letter and sound) and this has allowed us to play games away from the iPad such as 'Eye Spy' . . . The ABC dot-to-dot program has improved his handwriting skills as when he is writing now all he has to concentrate on is the pencil grip and posture. He is not constantly worried about how to form the letters as he knows where to start (top to bottom, left to right). He loves to write on his whiteboard with a large pen.

From these data it is clear that Sam had developed much in the way of basic written knowledge and skills through his use of educational apps on the iPad: the alphabet, phonemic awareness, grapho-phonemic relationships and letter formation. Moreover, this learning was transferable to other activities and platforms.

Jenny's mother likewise spoke of her daughter's love of educational apps. In addition to the phonics app, she highlighted language learning apps. Once again, her goals in for iPad use include English language learning along with reading development:

> She likes to do the literacy apps . . . and also she likes to do the app called Reading Egg. And she likes the vocabulary ones. You tap what they speak and then you tap the diagram as well.

Several of the children said they found the educational apps 'hard'. This was in response to a direct question about whether it was 'easy' or 'hard' to use the iPad. Nonetheless, the children were mostly positive about these apps and some nominated them as their favourite use of the iPad. In Chapter 1 we cited teacher data which indicated the excitement the children expressed to her when they successfully completed 'all the levels' of educational apps. One parent, though, said that her child found the apps 'tricky' and was somewhat discomforted when informed by the app that he was wrong and should start again.

In short, educational apps were well-received by the parents and the children. Notably, they were the only kind of app mentioned when the researcher asked the parents at the end of their first interview for suggestions of apps for the next phase of the project. In particular, the parents in these interviews requested apps for learning sight words, although there was mention also of apps for learning the alphabet, counting, numeracy, and problem-solving skills. It was apparent that these parents were seeking to better skill their children for the upcoming first compulsory year of schooling, known locally as 'Prep':

> I'd be happy for her to do a bit more letters and numbers, and, especially after seeing in Prep how much they are actually doing.

When encouraged to elaborate on their request for more educational apps, parents indicated that while it was good for the children to acquire the basic digital skills they would need in their worlds, basic print literacy skills were a priority. The teacher was not surprised by this position. She spoke of parents coming back to preschool and telling her about the 'Prep exam', an assessment of children's readiness administered by the school and of parents' concern about the number of sight words their children knew on entry into Prep. While she was happy to have educational apps on the iPads and encouraged children to use them during free play time at preschool (see Chapter 1), the teacher spoke of feeling some 'pressure' in this regard, and of some contradiction of her long-held epistemological position on literacy education at the preschool level.

Discussion and conclusions

From the data we have presented here it is clear that parents and the teacher were taking strategic positions on the goals of iPad-embedded literacy education. While there was a mixed response to the use of iPads for enriched reading experiences, participants were generally enthusiastic about the playful and productive communicative uses of the iPad promoted by the project. However, the structural reality of the national literacy assessment regimen saw some tempering of that enthusiasm. Although the children's first national literacy test was four years away, the accountability regimen was already shaping their literacy experiences: children were being directly prepared, to some extent in home and at preschool, for entry into the preparatory year of schooling.

In enabling us to get beyond the home/school and match/mismatch binaries, the epistemological analysis we have employed here (Compton-Lilly *et al.*, 2012) has provided a useful lens on the iPad loan programme. In addition, it prompts some questions about this family literacy initiative. With respect to participation, these relate to the under-representation of minority group parents in the programme. Did this reflect differences of epistemological position? Were the positions on the nature of literacy, the goals of literacy education, and the development and acquisition of literacy held by these parents different from those apparent in the project? What were their strategic decisions about the literacy education of their children? And what of the majority group parents who were not represented in the iPad loan programme? How did the epistemological position and educational strategy of the programme sit with theirs? These are questions worth pursuing in future practice and research. Our vision here is of home–school relations around the iPad – indeed, any literacy tool – that are negotiated, iterative and grounded in the complexities of the aspirations of families. On the part of teacher and researcher, critical reflexivity is required and an understanding of the epistemologies and strategies all bring to family literacy initiatives.

References

Australian Government Department of Education, Employment and Workplace Relations (2009). Belonging, being and becoming: The early years learning framework for Australia. Canberra: Commonwealth of Australia. https://www.coag.gov.au/sites/default/files/early_years_learning_framework.pdf Accessed March 30, 2014.

Brown, M. & Harmon, M.T. (2013). iPad intervention with at-risk preschoolers: mobile technology in the classroom. *Journal of Literacy and Technology*, 14(2), 56–78.

Burnett, C. (2010). Technology and literacy in early childhood educational settings: A review of research. *Journal of Early Childhood Literacy*, 10(3), 247–70.

Chiang, P.S. (2010). Home literacy education of Taiwanese Australian families: A sociological analysis. EdD thesis, QUT. http://eprints.qut.edu.au/43678/

Compton-Lilly, C., Rogers, R. & Lewis, T.Y. (2012). Analyzing epistemological considerations related to diversity: An integrative critical literature review of family literacy scholarship. *Reading Research Quarterly*, 47(2), 33–60.

European Commission (2014). Pillar VI: Enhancing digital literacy, skills and inclusion. http://ec.europa.eu/digital-agenda/en/our-goals/pillar-vi-enhancing-digital-literacy-skills-and-inclusion Accessed June 28, 2014.

Fisch, S.M., Shulman, J.S., Akerman, A. & Levin, G.A. (2002). Reading between the pixels: Parent-child interaction while reading online storybooks. *Early Education and Development*, 13(4), 435–51.

Hassett, D.D. (2006). Signs of the times: The governance of alphabetic print over 'appropriate' and 'natural' reading development. *Journal of Early Childhood Literacy*, 6(1), 77–103.

Heath, S.B. (1982). What no bedtime story means: Narrative skills at home and school. *Language in Society*, 11(12), 49–76.

Heller, M. (2008). Bourdieu and 'literacy education'. In J. Albright & A. Luke (eds), *Pierre Bourdieu and Literacy Education* (pp. 50–67). New York: Routledge.

Hill, S. & Nicholls, S. (2009). Multiple pathways between home and school literacies. In A. Anning, J. Cullen & M. Fleer (eds), *Early Childhood Education: Society and culture* (2nd edn) (pp. 164–84). Los Angeles, CA: SAGE.

Holdaway, D. (1979). *The Foundations of Literacy*. Sydney: Ashton Scholastic.

Hutchison, A., Beschorner, B. & Schmidt-Crawford, D. (2012). Exploring the use of the iPad for literacy learning, *The Reading Teacher*, 66(1), 16–23.

Kenner, C. (2000). *Home Pages: Literacy links for bilingual children*. Stoke-on-Trent: Trentham Books.

Larson, J. & Marsh, J. (2005). *Making Literacy Real: Theories and practices for learning and teaching*. London: Sage.

Luke, A. (1992). The body literate: Discourse and inscription in early literacy training. *Linguistics and Education*, 4(1), 107–29.

Marsh, J. (2003). One-way traffic? Connections between literacy practices at home and in the nursery. *British Educational Research Journal*, 29(3), 369–82.

Morgan, H. (2013). Multimodal children's e-books help young learners in reading. *Early Childhood Education Journal*, 41, 477–83.

Mu, G.L.M. & Dooley, K. (2014). Coming into an inheritance: Young adults' perceptions of family support and Chinese Heritage Language Learning,

International Journal of Bilingual Education and Bilingualism. DOI: 10.1080/13670050.2014.928258

Neumann, M.M. & Neumann, D.L. (2013). Touch-screen tablets and emergent literacy. *Early Childhood Education Journal*, 42, 231–9.

New London Group (1996). A pedagogy of multiliteracies: Designing social futures. *Harvard Educational Review*, 66(1), 60–92.

Northrop, L. & Killeen, E. (2013). A framework for using iPads to build early literacy skills. *The Reading Teacher*, 66(7), 531–37.

O'Mara, D. & Laidlaw, L. (2011). Living in the iworld: Two literacy researchers reflect on the changing texts and literacy practices of childhood. *English Teaching: Practice and Critique*, 10(4), 149–59.

Pahl, K. & Rowsell, J. (2005). *Literacy and Education: Understanding the new literacy studies in the classroom*. London: Paul Chapman Publishing.

Purcell-Gates, V. (ed.) (2007). *Cultural Practices of Literacy: Case studies of language, literacy, social practice, and power*. Mahwah, NJ: Lawrence Erlbaum Associates.

Roskos, K., Burstein, K. & You, B.Y. (2012). A typology for observing children's engagement with eBooks at preschool. *Journal of Interactive Online Learning*, 11(2), 47–66.

Rowsell, J. (2014). Toward a phenomenology of contemporary reading. *Australian Journal of Language and Literacy*, 37(2), 117–27.

Street, B. (1997). At last: Recent applications of New Literacy Studies in educational contexts. *Research in the Teaching of English*, 39(4), 417–23.

Street, B. (1984). *Literacy in Theory and Practice*. Cambridge: Cambridge University Press.

Taylor, D. (1983). *Family literacy: Young children learning to read and write*. Portsmouth, NH: Heinemann.

The State of Queensland (Queensland Studies Authority) (2010). Queensland kindergarten learning guideline. Brisbane: Queensland Studies Authority.

United States Government (2013). ConnectED Initiative. www.whitehouse.gov/issues/education/k-12/connected Accessed June 28, 2014.

Williams-Kennedy, D. (2009). Building bridges between literacies. In A. Anning, J. Cullen & M. Fleer (eds), *Early Childhood Education: Society and culture* (2nd edn) (pp. 91–102). Los Angeles, CA: Sage.

Chapter 8

Networking iPads into preschool spaces

Michael Dezuanni and Linda Knight

Introduction

In this chapter, we consider the introduction of iPads into the networked spaces of preschool classrooms, which involves complex relationships between children and adults, physical technology (iPads), virtual technology (wireless networks) and other materials such as desks and chairs, play stations, indoor and outdoor spaces, art and craft materials, toys, sandpits, smart boards, laptop computers, data projectors and storage devices. We argue that despite the accessibility of iPads as relatively easy devices to interact with, effectively networking them into preschool spaces is a complex process and requires consideration of the whole preschool 'ecology'. To make this claim, we draw on a range of data, including our observations of the teachers and children interacting with iPads in the preschools, interviews with the teachers, children and parents, recordings of planning and evaluation meetings and teachers' responses to survey questions. We employ actor–network theory (Fenwick & Edwards, 2010; Latour, 2005; Law, 2009) to demonstrate how the introduction of a new technology into preschool spaces has a broad range of consequences for learning, logistics, social dynamics and play. We consider examples of the implementation of the iPads in the three centres involved in the project to consider the ongoing negotiations that occurred between iPads, children and teachers mobilised by unexpected opportunities and challenges.

The first part of the chapter considers literature about ICTs in early years learning centres and we briefly introduce tensions reflecting broader social and cultural concerns about young children's use of digital technologies. Next we explain actor–network theory as an appropriate theoretical framework and argue it can elucidate the complex ways in which the introduction of a new technology such as the iPad creates a range of new ways for children to materially and conceptually participate in preschool spaces. The chapter then considers the 'actors' other than the children that constitute the networked relations of the preschool spaces: the iPads, the teachers and other 'things' such as toys, art and craft materials and furniture, as well as other technologies that support, extend and limit the use of the iPads. Through considering the preschool social and material network, we aim to investigate how the iPads become part of an overall system designed to promote play and learning.

ICTs in early years learning spaces

The arrangement of preschool learning spaces is generally mobilised by a play-based philosophy in which children are invited to interact with different materials, ideas and each other to play, learn and develop their social abilities (Dudek, 2000; Isbell & Evanshen, 2012). Preschool spaces typically differ to learning spaces made available to older children and adults because usually there is no centralised locus of learning, such as the front of the room, where the teacher stands at a whiteboard or lectern. Although preschools often have a zone where a teacher may gather the whole group, this is just one of many sites available to the children for learning with others including a variety of spatial zones inside and outside the preschool room(s). The preschools in our project included toy play zones, reading corners, model kitchen areas, music zones, maker spaces, technology tables/corners, semi-outdoor art and craft areas and outdoor play areas.

Technologies, including ICTs, have been present in many preschools for a substantial amount of time. Analogue technologies such as music records, cassette and CD players, televisions, slide projectors, overhead projectors, cameras and tape-based video cameras have all been available in preschools for many years. Desktop and laptop computers have also had a presence in preschools since at least the 1990s. According to Clements (1999), the ratio of computers to children in preschools in the United States in 1990 was 1:22, indicating that most preschools had at least one computer. In Scotland, Plowman and Stephen (2005) investigated the use of computers in preschool settings and found that 'playing with the computer' was a common activity for the children at all seven sites they investigated. These preschools were not identified as sites known for their computer use but were chosen for geographical, socio-economic and cultural representation. All seven centres included a computer and at six of the sites, children had daily opportunities to use a computer during free play times, although the children used the computers during instruction time at only one site, (p. 149). Brooker and Siraj-Blatchford (2002) conducted a study in what they describe as a 'typical' inner-urban nursery school in England catering for 3- to 5-year-olds, where a computer was available to be shared by the children and used as an integral part of the children's interactions and learning. Since the 1980s, a significant industry has also developed around 'learning software' that has aimed to capture the education market, including software designed for very young children (Ito, 2009, p. 29). In recent years, other digital technologies such as interactive whiteboards have also been introduced in many preschools.

In this context, tablet computers and apps are just the latest of different types of technologies that have been deployed in preschools in the past (see Siraj-

Blatchford & Whitebread, 2003). As we argued in Chapter 4, however, we believe iPads are a 'breakthrough' digital technology for preschools because the barriers to participation for young children are very low. The touch-screen interface, invisible file management process and simple menu system allow young children to use iPads with relative ease. In addition, the prevalence of the vast number of apps (both educational and entertainment-oriented) that may be used in preschool spaces makes tablets attractive devices, as does the inclusion of a digital camera and audio-recording capabilities. It is not surprising that iPads and other tablet devices are receiving attention in preschools. For instance, a recent online search for the phase 'iPads in preschools' returned 147,000 results, indicating a significant amount of discussion, commentary and accounts of the use of iPads with preschool-aged children, or in preschools. It seems possible tablet devices will become as common in preschools in the future as laptops and desktop computers have been in primary and secondary schools in recent decades.

Technology is not supported or present in all preschools, though, and there is a long history of resistance to the inclusion of technology in early years education, particularly digital technologies such as computers (Healy, 1998). A significant discourse in some approaches to preschool education supports the tradition originating with Jean-Jacques Rousseau that educational spaces should allow children to experience their senses and grow or flourish 'naturally' (Dudek, 2000, p. 43). Indeed, the German word *Kindergarten* (children's garden) is suggestive of a space infused with 'natural' nourishment and development. As indicated in the introduction to this book, the three preschools in our project were 'community kindergartens', although none of the teachers was opposed the inclusion of technology in their centres. A number of parents of the children in our project did, however, support a discourse of natural development for their children. For instance one response to the parent survey stated:

> I believe it is very important for children to experience their environment around them and to be tactile and that this is more soothing and therapeutic than staring at a screen – much better for their mental health to experience painting with a brush than drawing on the iPad.

This tension between 'natural' and 'technologised' childhoods consistently plays out whenever a new technology becomes available within popular culture and entertainment (Buckingham 2003). The recent proliferation of digital devices in family homes has led to concerns about 'screen time', lent weight by the American Academy of Pediatrics (2014) which recommends that children under two should have no screen time, and children and teenagers should be limited to no more than two hours of 'screen time' per day in total, including television, computers and touch-screen devices. In addition, they suggest 'that parents establish "screen-free" zones at home by making sure there are no televisions, computers or video games in children's bedrooms, and by turning off the TV during dinner'. These guidelines about exposure, particularly in relation to the very young, make preschools contested spaces when it comes to the introduction of digital technologies. Throughout this project, however, we saw little evidence that the iPads caused problems for the children in our study in relation to screen time, socialisation or opportunities to experience the senses. In fact, with much effort on the part of the teachers, the iPads become a resource with which to play, interact with other children and learn.

Actor–network theory

We turn to actor–network theory (Fenwick & Edwards, 2010; Latour, 2005; Law, 2009) in this chapter because it provides a productive way to think about the relationships that emerge when children, teachers, iPads, toys, books, apps, furniture, play equipment, the WiFi network, printers, art materials and other 'things' are brought together to coexist in preschool spaces. The somewhat surprising claim made by actor–network theory proponents is that both human and non-human 'actors' are able to shape what occurs in any 'actor–network' (Law, 2009). That is, a non-human 'actor', such as an iPad in a preschool space has a role to play in how the social situation of the preschool will be 'assembled', along with all other actors in the network. This is not to suggest the iPad can 'determine' human behaviour – actor–network theory refutes technological determinism, or the idea that technology can determine human behaviour. The focus is on the negotiations that take place when a child interacts with the iPad, or any other actor in the network. The benefit of deploying actor–network theory is that it helps to reveal the moments of negotiation that occur between actors and it leads to an understanding of why some things are possible in the network and others are not (Fenwick & Edwards, 2010). For instance, in Chapter 4, we discussed how the South Side preschool teacher became mobilised to introduce photography to the children because the iPads made available by the project included cameras. The two iPads previously available at South Side did not have cameras and they were mainly used as devices for reading interactive books and playing digital games; they were never taken outside or used for creative work. We can explain this change from an actor–network perspective by recognising how the availability of the cameras enrolled the teacher and children as photographers rather than as readers and players. The teachers and students were able to mobilise the iPad as a camera rather than as an eBook or gaming device.

Latour (2005, p. 108) describes the negotiations that occur between actors as opportunities for 'translation', which he describes as a relation that 'induces two mediators into coexisting'. The outcomes of this negotiation are dependent on the affordances/knowledge/ability of the actors involved. Callon (1986) argues there are key 'moments of translation' and in this chapter we will refer to two of these 'moments': enrolment and mobilisation. Enrolment exists when actors negotiate a relationship with each other. Mobilisation occurs at the moment when actors become 'manageable' and can be deployed for a purpose. In this chapter, we explore the various ways that different kinds of human and non-human actors in the preschools enrolled each other into relationships and how actors became mobilised for a purpose. It may seem strange to talk about a piece of furniture as an 'actor', but we hope it will become clear that even furniture has an important 'say' in what occurs with a technology like the iPad in a preschool space.

In the rest of this chapter, we will discuss three central actors or groups of actors established in the preschools through the introduction of the iPads for our project. We will not dedicate a section on children as actors in this chapter per se because the majority of this book describes the ways in which the children enrolled and mobilised the iPads for various purposes. As appropriate, however, we will discuss the children's role as they interacted with human and non-human actors in the network. The first actor to be discussed is the iPads and the ways in which they were deployed and mobilised by teachers and other adults with the intention that they assist children's learning. Next, we will discuss teachers as actors in the project because as they aimed to deploy the iPads they were in a constant process of negotiation with the iPad itself and the broader technological systems that the iPads relied upon. We will also discuss spaces and other materials the iPads came to coexist with in the preschools including furniture, storage, indoors and outdoors, art and craft materials and so on. Each of these is discussed in turn with reference to data generated throughout the project.

The iPad as an 'actor'

Throughout this book we have discussed how the children in our project played and learnt in various ways with iPads. In Chapter 4 we demonstrated how the children successfully operated the iPads and interacted with various apps to work with digital materials to communicate. In this chapter, we want to consider the relationship between the children and iPads as a process of negotiation, particularly the ways in which the children enrol and were enrolled by the iPads; and the ways in which they mobilised, and were mobilised, by the iPads. The relationship between children and iPads is not neutral but rather one in which children bring specific knowledge and abilities to the device. This knowledge and ability is not inherent within children and must be learnt and practised. Most of this book is about the specifics of how and what children learnt with iPads in our project and, therefore, the ways in which they performed a role in the actor–network. In this chapter, we will mostly focus on the affordances of the device and the ways in which the iPads were deployed in the preschools to invite the children to interact with and mobilise them in particular ways.

As a newly introduced resource in the preschools, the iPad is a central actor in our project. At the most fundamental level, the iPad is a digital mobile device with a touch-screen interface. As hardware, it differs significantly from other digital 'computing' technologies because it invites more tactile, fluid and mobile interaction. Unlike desktop computers, tablets are lightweight and are not encumbered with cords, keyboard and mouse that demand a desktop computer exists in a fixed location on a table or desk. Even though laptop computers are generally much more mobile than desktops, they are still most effectively interacted with at a desk, rather than on a lap (despite their name) and cannot be easily used for recording photographs or video footage. The camera on a laptop computer points directly at the person interacting with the laptop, rather than away from the computer and this invites the creation of particular types of images – for instance 'selfies' and video web streaming – rather than other types of photography and video production. The iPad's touch-screen interface seems to invite a more personal relationship with the device than desktop and laptop computers do. In domestic settings, iPads are often enrolled in leisure activities such as gaming, act as 'second screens' accompanying television viewing and are mobilised for everyday vernacular photography (Burgess, 2007). They are more likely than desktops and laptops to be interacted with in the lounge room, on a couch or at cultural, sporting or entertainment events. From this perspective, iPads enrol people to interact with them in many ways that desktop and laptop computers do not. The affordances of the iPad; its physical size and weight; its high-quality cameras, integrated into the device and pointing both toward and away from the person interacting with the iPad; and its smooth, tactile touch-screen interface invite versions of material and conceptual coexistence with people that are not common with desktop and laptop computers.

Despite the affordances of the iPads and the manner in which they enrol people to interact with them in domestic settings, in the early stages of our project, we saw children being invited to interact with them as if they were desktop or laptop computers. The teachers often arranged the iPads at a desk station and the children were able to rotate through the station to 'have a turn' on the iPads. In this sense, the teachers mobilised the iPads as if they were older style computers and as a consequence did not allow the children to fully negotiate the affordances of the iPads. Part of the reason for making the devices available in this centralised way was that it reflected how all the other zones and stations in the preschools were arranged and therefore how pedagogy was established and enacted in the centres. The South Side teacher explained her process for inviting the children to use the iPads at the beginning of the project – in technology corner – as one choice among several others:

> I'll say does anybody want to come and use the iPads today if there's nobody there. The same as I go there's room in block corner does anybody want to use block corner today or does, you know there's nobody at the easels is anybody interested in . . . They haven't gone there as much as I expected them to.

By enrolling the iPads into the established pedagogical pattern available in the centre, the teacher aimed to democratically treat the iPads in the same way that all other resources were treated. She wanted the children to experience the iPads as just another resource. In doing this, though, she initially limited the potential of the devices and the opportunities for children to play and learn with them. After some initial excitement, the children often had to be coaxed to visit the iPads in technology corner.

One reason for allowing the children to interact with the iPads through locating them in a zone was to protect the iPads from harm. The teacher at the South Side Centre had initial reservations about allowing the children to walk around with the iPads because she was concerned that they would be dropped and damaged. Early in the project she suggested that it might be better for the children to have access to iPad minis because she believed they would be easier for the children to hold, particularly for photography:

> after thinking about it for a little bit I thought perhaps maybe we should have had the mini-iPads, you know for the age group that they are, I was thinking maybe we should have gone for some tiny pads for their tiny hands.

As the project evolved, however, the teachers and researchers came to see that even very young children are capable of walking around with and simultaneously operating the iPads. For instance, the South Side teacher eventually realised the children were more adept at holding the larger iPads than she initially believed they would be. After completing a photography project, she reflected, 'I think they are really quite skilled at holding them and being able to hold and master taking photos so that has surprised me'. Part of the reason for the South Side teacher's new confidence was that she purchased 'big grip' cases and stands with the idea that the children would be able to grasp them more easily and that if they were dropped, the iPad would be less likely to be damaged (See Figure 8.1).

The South Side teacher was aware of the need to use the iPads in more creative ways than keeping them on a desktop, but she did not have the confidence to do this without modifying the iPads, stating, 'We need to start shifting them out of that technology corner and moving them around. As soon as I get my cases and I feel comfortable with them bouncing [laughter].' Each of the teachers in the preschools made decisions to customise the iPads to make them suitable for interaction with the children. In all the centres, covers were purchased for the iPads to protect them, although the covers were not always suitable because they sometimes obscured the camera and if the students wanted to record images, they had to remove the iPad from its case. All three centres also purchased headphones for use with the devices to make it easier for the children to hear in a noisy room. In these ways, the children and the teachers negotiated with the iPads as 'hardware' and the iPads were deployed

Figure 8.1 The iPad surrounded by a 'big grip' case

in the preschool spaces in quite specific ways as a result. To begin with, the teachers were hesitant to allow the iPads to be moved around the room and even as the project evolved, the children mostly needed quite a specific reason to be allowed to pick one up and take it to a different part of the room, or outside.

The iPads were also present as actors in the network through their file management system and their deployment of software in the form of apps. The file management system on a desktop or laptop computer can act as a significant barrier to interaction by young children because most file management systems rely on written text and complex navigation through menu and sub-menu systems. The menu system on the iPad is very simple, as the device centralises storage of all assets, including images, video footage, music and sound. Many apps enable access to all these assets and children do not have to name their files or find them buried in sub-menus and this dramatically simplifies negotiating the device and makes it relatively easy to creatively combine digital materials like photographs, audio and video footage. In this sense, the menu system makes it possible for the children to mobilise the iPad as a device for multimodal creativity. Most apps are also reasonably easy to navigate with simple three- or four-button menu systems, as described in Chapter 4. The children sometimes found it difficult, however, to navigate the sheer number of apps available on iPads and to make choices about enrolling one app over another to complete a specific task. When the teachers were asked what advice they would give teachers new to the iPad, they highlighted the need to carefully organise the apps into folders on the iPad so the children can easily find the ones they are looking for. The South Side teacher also mentioned throughout the project that she found it frustrating that the children would often skip from app to app, without spending what she considered to be a worthwhile amount of time with any one of them. She believed the iPad's 'openness' provided the children with too much freedom. She eventually found a solution to this through working out how to lock children into a specific app using 'guided access', which involves using 'accessibility' in the iPad's general settings. The teacher suggested this provided her with more control and flexibility in her curriculum planning because she could be certain the children were using the apps she wanted them to use. In this sense the teacher negotiated the iPad's openness and she was able to enrol the iPad to provide children the kind of educational experience she wanted to:

> Of course if a child wants to use a different app I can provide that for them individually but still prevent them from surfing all over the app selection and not finishing anything. I love it. I want my children to see the iPads as an educational tool not a gaming tool.

Apps on a touch-screen device seem to invite more direct interaction with children than software on a traditional computer does because to be deployed they simply have to be touched, tapped and swiped with a finger. Despite this simplicity of interaction, the touch-screen interface was sometimes a cause of frustration for the children. For instance, the North Side Centre teacher said the children sometimes became annoyed in the early stages of the project:

> There was a little bit of frustration with the children if they rested on something it wiped a screen . . . and with some of them they're pressing really hard to try and get it and it's just learning all of that sort of stuff.

These difficulties with young children's early physical interactions with the devices demonstrate that interacting with touch screens requires learning and practice. Once the students learnt to interact with the touch-screen interface, however, they very quickly seemed to be able to complete most of the various kinds of tasks enabled by the apps. One area this did not occur was with the virtual keyboard on the iPad as the children were only in the early stages of developing reading and writing knowledge and skills; where students wanted to include written text in their work, they typically enrolled significant teacher assistance. In general, though, the children in our project seemed to find the iPads easy to get along with and they worked with them to creatively communicate their ideas.

The teachers as 'actors'

The teachers played a key role in the actor–networks established through the introduction of iPads into the preschools. In this section of the chapter we discuss the ways in which the teachers negotiated the iPads as they attempted to manage the introduction of the devices into their preschools. We focus on the teachers' management of the logistics of allowing iPads into the preschool space; their attempts to integrate the iPads into the students' curriculum experiences; and the difficulties of managing the iPads as a technology. A key concern for the teachers at the beginning of the project was how to conceptualise the use of the iPads with the children when they had more immediate issues to deal with. For instance, all the teachers mentioned that a priority at the beginning of a new year is helping the children to develop social skills: introducing a new technology is not a priority, even if it is desirable. The following comment from the Outer North Side teacher was representative of this sentiment:

> Yes, so quite often we don't get a chance to get the iPads out to sit to show because we need to be with this child who needs help interacting, and with this child who needs help settling in, because they're brand new to the centre and they're a bit lost and they need help to make friendships.

One of the teachers also expressed concern about the idea that the children might stop interacting with other children if they interacted with the iPads by themselves and if it became difficult to move them away from the technology. Despite these concerns, the teachers also acknowledged that the iPads could assist the children to develop their social skills. For instance, the Outer North Side teacher mentioned that she could see how the children could socialise by taking photographs of each other. As the project went on, the teachers in all three centres cited examples of the children assisting other children with tasks on the iPads and generally spoke positively about the ways in which the iPads encouraged interaction between children.

The issue of protecting the iPads from the children also emerged in relation to the regular deployment of the devices in the centres. For instance, the Outer North Side teacher felt that some of the children could not be left alone with the devices and the iPads therefore became unavailable to the whole group: '. . . some children I couldn't trust to use them safely unsupervised. So they get kept in the office and we bring them out. But because you're not seeing them you sometimes forget that they're there'. Rather than being a regular presence in the preschool space, the iPads were therefore isolated in the teachers' office for their safekeeping, particularly in the early stages of the project. In this case the iPads were unharmed, but also unavailable. In this sense, they were enrolled as precious objects rather than as devices for children to play with and learn. The iPads were seen as a valuable resource in the preschools and the teacher at the South Side Centre was particularly concerned at the beginning of the project because they had experienced some break-ins at their centre. Although she wanted the iPads to be out and available in the preschool space, she did not want them to be visible to casual visitors or through the centre's windows, so she covered them with a large cloth. The South Side teacher also believed it was important for the children to recognise the iPads as a valuable resource, rather than just another toy to be played with: 'I think it was important that initially to start with they treat them with a great deal of respect and they learn what the, the rules of safety. How to keep them safe and how to look after them'. There was a clear negotiation, then, between the teachers, the iPads and the children around protecting the iPads from the children and allowing the children to enrol them in play and mobilise them for creativity and communication.

The teacher's capacity to manage the logistics of making the iPads available to the children became a significant problem during the project and the teachers regularly mentioned in interviews that one of their biggest difficulties was simply keeping track of the iPads and the children's use of them. At one of the evaluation days, one of the teachers said:

> Keeping track of ten or more iPads is really challenging. Loading updates, going through the data that has been collected, remembering which iPad was used in a particular incidence. Loading Dropbox, WiFi, email, [next words obscured by laughter] and then closing WiFi, Dropbox, email and removing data before iPads go home.

Some of the frustration mentioned by the teacher giving this account, accompanied by 'knowing' laughter from the other teachers, relates specifically to the preschool teachers' involvement in the research project. She mentions Dropbox because the teachers were asked to upload examples of student work as data artefacts to a remote folder and the iPads were allowed to 'go home' with the children as a specific aspect of the project and this placed an additional burden on the teachers to make sure the children's privacy was respected. Many aspects of this account, though, relate to the day-to-day management of the iPads, which would exist regardless of the research project. The South Side teacher designed a system to make it easier to keep track of which students were using the iPads and to allow the students to access the iPads from the storage system themselves, which saves her the time of having to put the iPads out each day, ready for the children to use:

> I'm just getting set up in the beginning of the day to do, you know, to prepare the room and to get everything ready that takes a lot of time to get them. I mean I've got to the point now where the children know, we've set up the drawers that the iPad is numbered . . . so they've learnt which iPad is theirs. They know now the drawers are numbered, they can go in if we don't put them out and they want to use one.

In a similar fashion, when asked to outline the biggest challenges in the project, the Outer North Side teacher drew attention to her already significant workload that extends far beyond contact time with the children:

> Like at the end of the day when you have to write up your program and answer all your emails and maybe write a few learning stories, to then have time to get out ten iPads and to try to synch them or to search for some apps. . . . I can't fit it in my day.

Likewise, the North Side teacher recounted how it was necessary for her and other teachers to take the iPads home a few at a time on a regular basis to make sure they were updated with the latest versions of apps and that they were clear of personal data if the children were to take them home. One solution being explored by at least two of the centres was to have parent volunteers assist with the management of the iPads, although to date this has not been successfully implemented.

A specific challenge for the teachers relates directly to the affordances of the iPad and its 'hidden' file management system. The iPads were designed as a personal device for the consumer market, rather than a device to be shared between individuals and they do not include a 'log in' system or create a personal profile or even a folder system where individual work can be stored. These choices are taken out of an individual's hands as the iPad stores all files centrally, and there is no option to name the files. As previously explained, this makes the iPad very accessible for children as they do not have to navigate complex menus, but the consequence is that there is no way to identify who completed the work on a specific iPad. The teachers managed this by allocating specific tablets to small groups of children, but this did not always solve the problem of identifying who had completed which work. This was especially challenging when the children took an iPad home where the teacher was not able to see the children using specific apps or creating particular artefacts. The South Side teacher explained:

> If I don't look at it the moment that it comes back in, in that next day and check what they did. Did they take photos, did they use apps? . . . There's no name on them unless they've written it with the pencil.

Writing their names with a 'pencil' refers to the students signing their name on their digital work, in the case of drawing apps, so that the teacher can see their name on the work, much as they would see it on a physical painting or drawing.

Teacher's negotiations with the iPads and associated technological systems were quite complex compared to the students' experiences of them. While the students interacted primarily with the iPads and various apps, the teachers were also required to interact with the Apple laptop supplied along with the iPads, the WiFi system in the preschool, printers, interactive whiteboards, the iTunes store and the vagaries of how different apps enable children's creations to be shared. For the teachers, the iPads were at the centre of a whole technological system that had to be negotiated and even though they were often successful in these negotiations, sometimes they were simply unable to make the system work for them. In this sense, their attempts to enrol and mobilise the iPads in particular ways sometimes failed. For instance, despite being very proficient with Windows on PCs, the Outer North teacher was not used to using Apple software and found it challenging to solve problems on the iPads:

> It frustrates me because I cannot figure out the things that take me two minutes on a PC take me 45 minutes on an iPad. I don't know where the buttons are and I don't know who to take troubles to, trying to get it from here onto the PC . . . it's just makes it difficult to load those things up.

She admitted that she simply gave up when it came time to print the students' work because it was too difficult to work out, despite her desire to allow the children to share their work with each other and their families. The South Side teacher also expressed frustration with the difficulties of printing from the iPads:

> I'm desperate to print those photography ones. I want to put up a display of what they've taken so yeah, it might be the school holidays before I actually get to fiddle with this and try it out and see whether it will actually recognise that printer.

Despite seeking professional help about how to have the iPads communicate with the preschool's newly purchased printer, the teacher was unable to solve the problem. The South Side teacher had also introduced a Mondopad interactive whiteboard into the preschool at the same time the iPads were introduced; she was having difficulty getting the Mondopad to recognise the iPads so she could display students' work directly from the iPads to the Mondo Board. Sharing and displaying children's work with other children, parents/caregivers and visitors is a central aspect of preschool curriculum objectives and teachers' established pedagogic practices, so the difficulties the teachers experienced with this aspect of the project were particularly frustrating. In addition to the problems of printing and linking with displays such as the Mondo Board, the teachers found that some of the apps they used did not present an effective way to 'export', to share children's work in a regular file format. For instance, some apps only presented sharing through an online service like YouTube, Facebook or another 'cloud based' service, which was not practical or desirable in a preschool setting. Sometimes, the app wanted to share the file as an 'epub', as was the case with the popular Book Creator app. The problem with epubs from the preschools' perspective was that parents would not have the software to view the epub file on their computer. Although it was possible to export a PDF from Book Creator, many of the interactive features of the production were then lost. At the North Side Centre, the teachers devised a work-around for some apps when they used the iPad's screen capture function, to send still images of student work to the iPad's photo reel. This solution, however, still did not capture multimedia aspects of a production.

In addition to difficulties with sharing students' work, the North Side Centre teachers also had to negotiate with their centre's slow WiFi speeds, which made it difficult to easily download an app or digital story; the only solution was to take the iPads home where faster data speeds were available. The North Side Centre also experienced unpredictable technological issues. At one point, one of their iPads froze and the iPad had to be taken to the Apple store to be fixed. Although the store assistant was easily able to fix the problem, she explained that it was due to an obscure 'glitch' related to iCloud backup systems. This last example points to the unpredictability of the kinds of challenges the teachers had to negotiate to introduce the iPads into their centres. It also shows that no matter how much professional development teachers can access, technical issues will always present obstacles and unless the teachers have the time, skills and knowledge to stay abreast of all the latest iPad developments, they are likely to encounter problems at some stage. The iPad may be easy for children to interact with, but its reliance on regular technological upgrades from Apple and the vagaries of specific apps ensures teachers' negotiations with the device are not without difficulty. Despite all this, the teachers all spoke very highly about the possibilities for the iPads in their preschools and seemed to be willing to keep trying to solve technical issue to make the iPads available to the children.

Other actors in the preschool spaces

When the iPads were introduced into the preschools for our project, they entered a space for young children that was already rich with opportunity for play and learning and in which children had many opportunities to interact with each other, their teachers and a host of other material and conceptual 'actors' competing for their attention. The teachers in each centre put a great deal of consideration into the curriculum experiences available to the children and aimed to ensure they had access to stimulating and interesting resources. The teachers were all convinced, though, that it was important for the children to have access to digital technologies, because as one teacher said, 'We are in a technological world that changes constantly and rapidly. The changes are obvious to us as adults, the children see it as their "normal". We need to understand their world and know how to best support them'. All the teachers also agreed that the iPads should complement the children's preschool experiences rather than replace them. The teachers pointed to other 'actors' (our word, not theirs) in the preschools that they believed the children should interact with, including pencils for the development of fine motor skills, and art and craft materials to have hands-on, tactile experiences. As one teacher said in the initial survey when asked to comment on the role of digital devices alongside other materials and resources:

> They are all tools that should be used in conjunction with each other. Like all learning, children will have preferences in their learning styles and for the tools they choose. The more options we can provide the better outcomes we can expect to see, as children will find another way not previously available.

As we have already noted in this chapter, although the iPads provide another 'thing' for children to play with and learn, they have affordances that are likely to be limited by placing them in isolation away from other toys, materials, technologies, books and spaces in the preschools. Placing them in isolation ensures that the children can only interact with the iPads as a device for playing games-based apps, eBooks, drawing apps and screen content such as videos and television shows. For instance, it is difficult for the children to mobilise the cameras on the iPads to record images of play taking place in other zones. The South Side teacher recognised the need to move the iPads away from technology corner as the project went on and once the issue of the iPads' safety was resolved, the devices were used more frequently by the children for photography, as outlined in Chapter 1. The teacher was, however, adamant that the iPads should never entirely replace a non-digital activity. As she explained:

> We never substitute them [iPads] for something, if we use them we use a hand-held material as well, so they're drawing on them we're going to put them out on that table where they do their drawing and get a paper and they can choose whether they use that or the iPad.

It is important to the South Side teacher – and the other teachers in the project generally agreed with this point – that children continue to have tactile experiences of the 'real' world and that the digital world they are invited to take part in via the iPads involves ongoing non-digital experiences. From this perspective, the other well-established 'things' in the preschool space are valued partly because they are bodily and sensory and involve the deployment of material items to participate through physical 'doing'. There is a sense that holding a pencil or paintbrush, feeling paint in between your fingers, feeling the weight of an item, building something with physical building blocks or dressing up in real clothes matters a great deal to children's development. It is unclear from the data if the iPad itself is recognised as a material item to be physically experienced by the children. Most of the discussion seemed to position the iPad as a virtual or digital item. As we argued in Chapter 4, though, the materiality of the iPad matters for the development of digital media literacies and as Marres (2012) suggests, technological items can be central to 'material participation' and getting real things done.

Although none of the teachers was explicit about the status of iPads as material items to be played and experimented with alongside other material items, the South Side teacher seemed to recognise this through the photography project the children took part in and in which the teacher suggests the iPads became 'just another tool in the room'. This was most explicitly demonstrated through an activity in which children were encouraged to consider the texture of various items around the preschool and then take close-up images of the items to visually record these textures. The teacher explained how she thought about this idea for a classroom activity when she was in a park on the weekend and she came across some beautiful trees and she felt the need to feel the texture of the trees' bark. She then felt compelled to take an image of the trees and she went back to her car and accessed an iPad to record images of the trees. The following week she decided she would get the children to do something similar in the preschool. In this sense, the teacher enrolled the children into tactile relationships with different items in the preschool and then had them mobilise the iPads to record images, in part to preserve the memory of the texture so that it becomes not just a tactile experience, but a visual one that reminds the children of their bodily experience. By bringing the iPads into coexistence with the children and other items in their physical environment, the teacher helps the children to materially participate in their environment in a way that would otherwise not be available to them. As the project evolved, the South Side teacher continued to bring the iPads into the centre of preschool activity to integrate it into the other activities taking place. Figure 8.2 captures a sense of this as the teacher sits in group zone with the children's artworks hanging in the background, with an open art book beside her and an art app on the iPad, which she is explaining to the children.

The book sitting open beside the teacher in this image draws attention to another relationship negotiated between the iPads and other items in the preschool spaces – between physical books and books available on the iPads. All the teachers agreed that eBooks and iBooks should not replace physical books and, as discussed in Chapter 1, the South Side teacher made a decision that where possible only iBooks with an accompanying physical book should be made available to the children. In response to the initial teacher survey, one of the teachers said:

> I still think there is something magical about books. The feel and texture of the paper, the smell of old books, sharing a story with a teacher, friend or family member, it seems so much more special than watching a screen.

This response creates a powerful image that reflects a romantic ideal about how adults should help books to enrol children as readers and storytellers. This ideal child reader seems at risk from the seductive powers of the iPad and other

Figure 8.2 The South Side teacher demonstrating an art app

screen technologies and there has been considerable public discourse about the need to preserve books for children (Battersby, 2013). The preschool teachers, particularly the South Side teacher, seemed to view interaction with iPads as an opportunity to encourage children to interact with traditional books. As researchers, we were keen to explore the possibilities of teachers using iBooks for reading with children and developing children's understandings of storytelling, but these were not activities for which the iPads were often deployed. Furthermore, we generally did not see children sitting by themselves on beanbags or in the reading corner interacting with iPads in the way they would interact with books. The children often seemed to 'view' iBooks with other children rather than read them alone. Or if they read the iBooks by themselves, they sat at a desk with their headphones on so they could hear the narrative in a noisy room. When teachers wanted to engage the students as a group with reading, they mostly continued to use traditional books.

Conclusion

In this chapter we discussed ways in which the iPads became networked into preschool spaces and came to coexist with a range of other human and non-human 'actors'. This has allowed us to think about the complex negotiations that take place as these actors enrol and mobilise each other to perform particular tasks and solve certain problems. We argued that iPads have a range of affordances that invite children to interact with them in ways that other computers like desktops and laptops cannot and we argued that children generally find the iPads easy to 'get along with' as they communicate and create using both digital and non-digital materials. As actors in the network, the teachers were involved in complex negotiations with pedagogic practices, familiar classroom routines, curriculum requirements, existing classroom materials, parents' expectations, the children's needs, concerns for the safety of the iPads and the broader technological systems existing around the iPads. A key negotiation was about the mobility and safety of the iPads, but ultimately the teachers chose to allow the children to pick them up off the tables and mobilise the iPads to use them for photography, audio recording and video production. The teachers became more confident, that, at least if the iPads had protective covers, the iPads were robust and could stand up to a certain movement around the preschools in the hands of the children. This led to pedagogic practices that are impossible if the devices remain deskbound. Perhaps most importantly, once the iPads were allowed to be mobile, they were able to genuinely interact with the children and a range of other 'actors' in the preschools. This allowed the devices to work alongside and as part of the children's artwork, their storytelling and communication. The iPads became mobilised by the children not just as gaming devices or screens to view film and television content; rather, they became multimodal production devices and we believe this enabled the development of literacy and creativity in ways that were otherwise unavailable to the children.

References

American Academy of Pediatrics (2014). *Media and Children*. www.aap.org/en-us/advocacy-and-policy/aap-health-initiatives/Pages/Media-and Children.aspx Accessed June 18, 2014.

Battersby, L. (2013). Technology no Substitute for reading time: Mem Fox. *Sydney Morning Herald*. www.smh.com.au/digital-life/digital-life-news/technology-no-substitute-for-reading-time-mem-fox-20131109–2x8dw.html Accessed June 27, 2014.

Brooker, L. & Siraj-Blatchford, J. (2002) 'Click on Miaow!': How children of three and four years experience the nursery computer. *Contemporary Issues in Early Childhood*, 3(2), 251–73.

Buckingham, D. (2003). *Media Education: Literacy, learning and contemporary culture*. Cambridge: Polity Press.

Burgess, J. (2007). *Vernacular creativity and new media* (unpublished doctoral dissertation). QUT, Brisbane.

Callon, M. (1986). Some elements of a sociology of translation: Domestication of the scallops and the fishermen of St Brieuc Bay. In J. Law (ed.), *Power, Action, Belief: A new sociology of knowledge*. London: Routledge and Kegan Paul.

Clements, D.H. (1999). Effective use of computers with young children. In J.V. Copley (ed.), *Mathematics in the Early Years* (pp. 119–28). Reston, VA: National Council of Teachers of Mathematics.

Dudek, M. (2000). *Kindergarten Architecture: Space for the imagination*. London: Spon Press.

Fenwick, T. & Edwards, R. (2010). *Actor–network Theory in Education*. London: Routledge.

Healy, J. (1998). *Failure to Connect*. New York: Simon & Schuster.

Isbell, R. & Evanshen, P. (2012). *Real Classroom Makeovers: Practical ideas for early childhood classrooms*. Lewisville, TX: Gryphon House.

Ito, M. (2009). *Engineering Play: A cultural history of children's software*. Cambridge, MA: MIT Press.

Latour, B. (2005). *Reassembling the Social: An introduction to actor–network theory*. Oxford: Oxford University Press.

Law, J. (2009). Actor Network Theory and Material Semiotics. In B.S. Turner (ed.), *The New Blackwell Companion to Social Theory* (pp. 141–58). Chichester: Wiley-Blackwell.

Marres, N. (2012). *Material Participation: Technology, the environment and everyday publics*. New York: Palgrave Macmillan.

Plowman, L. & Stephen, C. (2005). Children, play, and computers in preschool education. *British Journal of Educational Technology*, 36(2), 145–57.

Siraj-Blatchford, J. & Whitebread, D. (2003). *Supporting ICT in the Early Years*. Berkshire: McGraw-Hill Education.

Conclusion

This book has aimed to share what we have learnt about the use of iPads for literacy and creativity development with 3- and 4-year-old children in three preschools in Brisbane, Australia. In this chapter, we provide a summary of our explorations and propose a set of strategies for the authentic and meaningful use of iPads with young children in formal education settings, which we present as 'digital basics'. We have arrived at this set of five digital basics through identifying key themes that emerged across the eight chapters of the book. We end the chapter by discussing what we think requires our attention next as we move forward with a new phase of our research about the use of iPads and other mobile digital devices in preschool settings.

The book's first chapter provided examples from the South Side preschool showing how the iPads were able to become part of authentic literacy events, particularly through children's development of story and scientific literacies. We outlined examples of the children using the iPads as a digital listening post for story reading and as a platform for creating multimodal stories. The iPads were also used for reading scientific websites and for creating multimodal science posters. A major challenge for the teacher, though, was that this type of work required significant amounts of time, often one-on-one guidance, and it simply was not always possible for the teacher to be available to the children in this way in a play-based environment. Paucity of time was also a significant issue discussed by teachers in both the other preschools in the project. Despite the iPads and most apps being relatively simple for the children to use with initial adult guidance, the sheer number of iPad features and available apps is daunting for both the children and teachers. When this is coupled with the complex work of supporting the development of children's authentic literacies across modes and forms, teachers are presented with a significant, multi-layered pedagogic challenge. One response to this was for the South Side teacher to lock the children into one specific app at a time with which they are familiar; and another was to enlist the assistance of other adults, particularly volunteer parents and caregivers. A three-tiered planning process that identifies and prioritises hardware operation, app operation, and literacy content needs and goals may also be useful.

In Chapter 2, we argued that the iPad is exemplary of young children's increasing engagement with digital technologies in post-industrial societies and that this presents both opportunities and challenges for arts education. We focused on three tensions that emerged as themes across the three preschools. The first tension is between the digital and the 'real' and adults' concerns that children should have opportunities to have tactile, sensory and bodily experiences of the world. Arts educators and practitioners also argue for the need to interact with digital technologies for creativity, but that this should not supplant corporeal experience and expression. This chapter and others presented examples where the children were encouraged to use the iPads to add creative layers to their non-digital work, for instance through taking photographs of paintings and then remixing them on the iPad. The second theme to emerge in Chapter 2 was that teachers believed it was important for children to create original works using the iPads rather than use them only for interacting with games-based and story reading apps. The third theme supports the point made in Chapter 1 in relation to literacy development: that for children to develop their creativity with the iPads they require significant adult assistance.

Using the iPads for drawing and writing on the screen was the focus of Chapter 3, which argued that the children in the project were highly motivated to use the iPad and that the bright colours on the screen encouraged children to persist with performing writing and drawing tasks, which they did by using their finger as a stylus. The chapter suggests children's confident use of fine motor skills shows how technology can actively support motor skill development and contest conventions about how children learn to draw and write. The project suggests a significant advantage of the iPad over the use of physical materials for drawing is that children can easily undo their work if they are not happy with it and this seems to encourage experimentation. It is also an advantage that children who may avoid drawing in conventional modes may be willing to draw on the iPads. The chapter also argued that educators used particular pedagogical approaches with the iPads, such as direct teaching, to introduce the children to new apps. Explicit instruction and using the correct terminology for apps and functions helped the children understand, experiment and successfully produce digital art works.

Chapter 4 outlined a 'building blocks' framework that includes *digital materials* and *media concepts* as knowledge domains and *media production* and *media analysis* as processes for children's development of digital media literacies with the iPads. The chapter builds on work within the media literacy field that aims to enable children to successfully participate in digital contexts through creative production and critical reflection. We suggested the development of digital media literacies is important in post-industrial contexts where children engage with commercial transmedia products in complex ways. The chapter shows how children in our project used the iPad as a media production device to communicate through the creation and combination of digital materials using apps; including photographs, video footage, audio recordings and drawings. We argued that for the children to communicate effectively, it was necessary for them to consider media concepts like multimodal language, such as shot types and camera angles, as well as audience and representation. We concluded that the 3- and 4-year-olds in our project were capable of storytelling through media production.

The children's storymaking/storytelling with iPads was investigated in more depth in Chapter 5, specifically through the notion of 'digital liveness' within a drama education framework. We suggested digital liveness could describe some of the creative activity children undertook in the project, particularly as they engaged with the iPads and apps through live and digital intermedial processes to make stories. For instance, while the children's creative work with apps like Puppet Pals cannot strictly be characterised as drama, the children worked on story elements central to dramatisation as they interacted with characters in real time on the screen. The chapter presents four key ideas for practice in preschools that might be considered when using an iPad and selected apps for storymaking events with children. These include making time for questioning and reflection in storymaking activities; engaging with apps that provide opportunities to develop oral literacy; using apps that allow for multi-sensory engagement on both the iPad and with non-digital materials; and selecting apps that provide children with opportunities to experience agency.

In Chapter 6, we located children's art making with the iPads within broader public discourses about the value and worth of art in Western cultures and children's art, in particular. We gave particular attention to the romanticisation of children's art in some of the dominant traditional and progressive educational approaches to art education. A risk of these approaches as they play out in preschool spaces is that they may not challenge normative and non-reflexive approaches that suggest art is important in education because it is somehow 'good' for children (rather than being an opportunity to disrupt or challenge norms, for instance); that art is a solitary, almost sacrosanct activity; and that making art necessarily fires the imagination and is best practised with certain acceptable materials. We argued that making art on the iPad has the potential to challenge these norms because it involves different processes. The chapter discusses children making art with several different apps and discusses the affordances of these apps in terms of the opportunities they provide children to develop their creative knowledge and skills. We also discuss some of the tensions that arose between digital and non-digital work and the ways in which these were prioritised by teachers and parents/caregivers. The chapter concludes that the iPad provides important opportunities for children to develop aesthetic knowledge in digital contexts.

Chapter 7 looked at home–school relations around the iPad through an account of the iPad loan programme built into the project. Drawing on recent scholarship in the field of family literacy, we undertook an epistemological analysis of the programme, focusing on the programme itself and family use of book apps, creating apps and educational apps. We showed that our goal of promoting enriched storytimes and playful, productive communication met with mixed success. Creating apps were embraced more enthusiastically in some cases than book apps; moreover, educational apps, which were not a major emphasis of the programme, were received with particular enthusiasm. We highlighted the multiplicity of epistemological positions at work in the design and enactment of the programme; we noted nuances of strategy as parents, teachers and researchers grappled with somewhat competing demands in a paradoxical environment where print basics are being institutionalised more deeply in schooling even as the need for digital basics becomes inescapable.

In Chapter 8, we focused on the ways in which the iPad came to coexist with people and other materials and items in the preschool spaces and the negotiations that were required for children and teachers to be able to interact with them in productive ways. We found that the affordances of the iPad make it a relatively accessible computer device for children to play and learn with. On the other hand, teachers had to do an enormous amount of negotiation with the iPads, the broader technologies that supported the iPads and the wider preschool space and materials and this presented many challenges. In particular, the teachers had to negotiate their existing pedagogical arrangements as these were not always conducive to making the most of the iPads and they had to learn to be less protective of the iPads. The teachers had to learn how to negotiate the large number of apps available for the iPads and invent ways of managing these resources for the children to be able to use them. The teachers were particularly challenged by a range of technological and network barriers, inexplicable glitches and a lack of time to manage the iPads efficiently. Despite all this, the teachers were adamant having the iPads in their preschools was a positive experience and that they were slowly adapting their presence.

'Digital basics' and mobile digital technologies in preschools

As we suggested in the introduction to this book, one of the objectives of our project was to explore the digital literacy opportunities young children might experience in preschool to assist them to participate successfully in the first years of formal schooling. We particularly wanted to identify the ways in which children's literacy and creativity could be developed when a technology like the iPad was introduced. The 'digital basics' presented below are not intended as a checklist; rather, they are strategies for designing learning experiences for children to allow them to begin to develop literacy and creativity in digital contexts. We acknowledge that these strategies are contingent on teachers having time and resources. We are not suggesting that these 'basics' must be present at all times for preschools to successfully implement iPads or other tablet technologies. Rather, they are presented as a map to help teachers navigate their way through the challenges of introducing mobile digital technologies in preschool spaces.

Digital basic one – authentic literacies and creativity

It goes without saying that children should have authentic learning experiences when interacting with iPads that begin to develop their knowledge and skills to successfully participate in digital culture. Many apps that purport to develop literacy and creativity, though, provide children with didactic learning experiences having little to do with children's life worlds. During our project, children often chose to ignore apps that provided them with no opportunity to create their own content or participate in ways that appealed to them. Some game-based apps engaged the children for a small amount of time, but soon became uninteresting. Children seemed to have the most authentic experiences when they were able to pick the iPads up from the table and use them to take photographs, record their voices and use apps to combine these materials. In particular, making stories in a range of forms allowed the children to participate with the iPads in meaningful ways. Authentic literacy and creativity often involved using the multimodal features available on the iPads.

Digital basic two – digital pedagogies

Children in our project also experienced the iPads in authentic ways when the teachers adjusted their pedagogies to allow the children to interact with them in a range of ways, rather than centralising them in an iPad zone or technology corner. Rather than conceptualising the iPads as another location to visit, the teachers explained that they were more satisfied with the children's use of the iPads when they were used as a resource to complement a range of other activities. For instance, when the iPads were taken to the art easels at the South Side preschool, the children took photographs of their artwork and then added further layers of creativity to their work. When the children at Outer North Side were encouraged to design a new outdoor play space, they were able to use the iPads to communicate their design ideas visually and orally. These are instances of digital pedagogy because they allow the children to make the most of the affordances of the iPads and apps. We make a distinction here between mere digitalisation of print-based pedagogies (e.g. the digital listening post) and digital pedagogy that realises the multimodal and interactive potential of tablet hardware and software and the collaborative learning ways that are normalised in digital culture.

Digital basic three – digital media literacies

In post-industrial societies in which children engage in digital culture, they regularly interact with commercial transmedia franchises as a central part of their play. We have argued that the children in our project were able to develop digital media literacies with the iPads by assembling knowledge through *digital materials* and *media concepts* and through the processes of *media production* and *media analysis*. These 'building blocks' of digital media literacy allow children to begin to participate as reflective media producers and consumers in digital culture. The iPad's affordances make it an accessible device with which young children can learn the operational/material and conceptual knowledge to become media producers. We suggest digital media literacies as a strategy for the use of iPads because we believe children should have opportunities to participate in digital culture through both making and critically reading media products.

Digital basic four – converged play and learning

In almost every chapter in this book teachers' and caregivers' desire to protect children's continued tactile, sensory and bodily experiences with toys, paper-based books, art materials and other equipment while using the iPads was raised. This was especially strong in relation to the aural and tactile experience of storybook reading. Throughout the project, however, we saw little evidence that children favoured entirely digital experiences for play and learning. Indeed, teachers reported that few students in any of the preschools had to have their iPad time limited – most children wanted to spend time doing other things throughout the day as well as interact with the iPads. Many of the most interesting activities undertaken by the children, though, were 'converged' activities in which the children merged non-digital and digital materials. These activities were also authentic in the sense that they allowed the children to explore their play and social interactions through the iPads.

Digital basic five – networking digital technologies

On a pragmatic level, one of the biggest challenges faced by the teachers in our project was dealing with the technological system surrounding the iPads and managing the children's projects on the iPads. All three teachers indicated that their lives would have been much easier had a number of technological challenges been solved for them. The teachers often found it difficult to share children's work from particular apps, for instance by printing directly from the iPads; it was difficult for the teachers to keep the iPads updated; software glitches sometimes came along that they were unable to solve and so on. In addition, the iPad's hidden file management system made it difficult to keep track of individual children's work. A key recommendation from this project is that the introduction of iPads or any other digital device into a preschool space requires a significant amount of practical systems planning. It is crucial to put thought into how best to set up devices in a space to allow children to successfully interact with them and to make life easier for the teachers.

Where to from here?

For us, the study this book reports on has been the beginning of an ongoing project to understand how digital mobile devices like the iPad can be used for children's literacy and creativity development in preschool settings. We have learnt a great deal from our investigations, but it would be productive to be able make adjustments to the methodology, building on what we now know. For instance, it would be useful to trial a digital technologies kit in preschools, consisting of iPads, along with a laptop, compatible printer, smart board and other applicable devices to explore if it is possible to solve some of the technological issues the teachers faced. As Android- and Windows-based tablets become more common in preschool settings, we would like explore the similarities and differences in the ways they are deployed by teachers. We would like to further explore the concept of authenticity and what it means for 3- and 4-year-old children living in post-industrial digital cultures. We would also like to give more thought to the idea of converged play and learning and further explore children's work that combines digital and non-digital materials. Finally, our study has been limited to three suburban preschools and we would, ideally, continue our exploration in regional, rural and remote areas of Australia to help address some of the specific digital inclusion challenges for children, families and preschools in those diverse communities. In designing such a study we would seek parental input on family literacy components from the outset in order to identify epistemological and strategic synergies and tensions within and between home and preschool.

As we write this book, many schools in our part of the world are starting to grapple with the concept of 'bring your own device' (BYOD) as an approach to technology provision for education. The BYOD approach is attractive to schools and education systems because some of the cost of technology provision is shifted to students and their parents/caregivers. Our research on the use of iPads in preschools suggests BYOD is likely to lead to even more complex networks as different kinds of devices with different affordances, pedagogical requirements and demands on teachers emerge. An important outcome of our project is that it matters what kind of device is used for literacy and creativity development because each device and its associated software has its own affordances that invite children to interact with it in specific kinds of ways. We do not know if BYOD with be successful or not, in terms of allowing children and young people to have greater access to digital devices at school. We can confidently suggest, though, that the development of literacy and creativity through digital devices will only occur where the kinds of strategies outlined in our 'digital basics' are attended to, providing children and young people with meaningful learning opportunities.

Index

bold = extended discussion or word highlighted in text;
b = box; f = figure; n = endnote or footnote; t = table.

For Product Safety Concerns and Information please contact our EU representative GPSR@taylorandfrancis.com
Taylor & Francis Verlag GmbH, Kaufingerstraße 24, 80331 München, Germany

www.ingramcontent.com/pod-product-compliance
Ingram Content Group UK Ltd.
Pitfield, Milton Keynes, MK11 3LW, UK
UKHW011015180926
475701UK00004B/763
9781138219731